Your Pain Is Showing*!*

Your Pain Is Showing!

Attitude, Patience And Paradigms

...and how to change them when they go bad

By L.F. Low

Zoë*life*
Publishing

Zoëlife
Publishing
900 N League Road
Colfax, IA USA 50054

Copyright © 2011 L.F. Low

Printed in the United States of America on acid free paper by
www.createspace.com.

Cover by Andrew Spurlin / Detroit Lakes, Minnesota
Edited by Daryl Jung / Toronto, Ontario, Canada

Low, L.F.
Your Pain Is Showing! / by L.F. Low

Includes bibliography and index.

ISBN-13: 978-1452857022
ISBN-10: 1452857024
1. Body, Mind & Spirit 2. Christian life
I. Title
Set in Garamond

All rights reserved. No part of this book may be reproduced or transmitted in any form or by any means, electronic or mechanical, including photocopying, recording, or by any information storage and retrieval system, without permission in writing from the Publisher.

For Dixie

My wife of 46 years, who has loved me, stood beside me and encouraged me for as long as we have known each other (over 50 years now). After 18 years of marriage it was all but over — I had become so controlled and driven by my fears that I was miserable to live with. At times, I was outright cruel. But Dixie hung in there and allowed me to learn how to follow God, love my wife and be a father to my children. Now I am a contented grandfather of 16 who, by the way, all love me. And what of Dixie? Well, we love each other absolutely and look forward to our next 50 years together.

Thank you, dear Dixie!

"The work of righteousness will be peace, and the effect of righteousness, quietness and assurance forever."
(Isaiah 32:17)

Your Pain Is Showing!

Contents

Forward/Editor's Note..............................*vi*
Preface/Author's Note...........................*viii*
Dedication...*xi*
Introduction..*1*

PART I /Attitude

Chapter One
Attitude Is A Big Deal..............................10
Chapter Two
Attitude Vs. Aptitude...............................15
Chapter Three
Existence And Enlightenment....................31
Chapter Four
Spiritual Or Psychological?.......................39
Chapter Five
Undergoing Metamorphosis.......................45
Chapter Six
Communicating With God........................49
Chapter Seven
Transformation, An Altar Experience.............57

Chapter Eight
Pulling Down Strongholds…….....................…….64
Chapter Nine
Casting Down Arguments…………….....…..69
Chapter Ten
Capturing Thoughts……………………………..72

PART II / Paradigms

Chapter Eleven
Purpose And Paradigms……………………...77
Chapter Twelve
Swallowing Pride………………………….…..86
Chapter Thirteen
Bearing Criticism, Taking Advice……………...94
Chapter Fourteen
Paying Due Respect………………………....101
Chapter Fifteen
Accepting Authority…………………....……109
Chapter Sixteen
Living Love……………………………..114
Chapter Seventeen
Winning At Work………………………….118
Chapter Eighteen
Family Matters……………………...…….122
Chapter Nineteen
Sex And The Christian……………………….131

PART III / Patience

Chapter Twenty
The Old Mirror Test..................................142
Chapter Twenty-One
Judging Others..147
Chapter Twenty-Two
Correcting Others......................................150
Chapter Twenty-Three
Righting Wrong..154
Chapter Twenty-Four
Divinely Human.......................................157
Chapter Twenty-Five
Adjusting Attitude....................................163
Chapter Twenty-Six
Trusting God..167
Chapter Twenty-Seven
The Next Step..173
Chapter Twenty-Eight
Fear Of Confrontation..............................179
Chapter Twenty-Nine
Dealing With Anger.................................183
Chapter Thirty
Forgiveness From The Heart....................187
Conclusion..192
Appendix One
Pinpointing Pain......................................194
Appendix Two
Finding Forgiveness................................203
Appendix Three
Testimonies...209
  From Drugs To Living In Peace...............209

Tourette's, Panic Gone For Good....................210
From Hatred, Abuse To Love, Peace.................211
Reference
Bibliography...213
Index
Key Words And Phrases.............................215
About The Author......................................220
About The Editor 222

Forward/Editor's Note

When the goodly Pastor Larry F. Low and my (in some ways, similar) paths first crossed at his place of employ, he was on a small roll and I was in a big hole – each of our own making.

As he was riding high and dry, discovering his passion for pencil-pushing his message – of God's perfect peace – to all the people, while guiding his current herd of bent young men toward redemption, I was being beaten down, to a complete existential and emotional pulp, by mad forces beyond my control.

In spite of it all we connected. I was incredulous and adrift amid the demonstrative machinations of Evangelical fundamentalism, and Pastor Larry had my back big-time. He knew I was in shock.

I had to flee that scene fairly quickly, obviously. But first I edited a letter (of his) to the editor of the local broadsheet, and he got a byline on the lead story with a nice pic of his mug atop the op-ed page.

So it became clear that good ol' God had sent me down there (as turns out, for just this one reason) to team up, in some fashion, with this Larry fella. He rode a big bike to work. He was clearly a cut above.

True, we are on polar-opposite ends of the earth theologically, philosophically and politically.

Yet Pastor L did not then (even though I was just off my second-to-last booze cruise, rightly resenting everything in sight), and does not now, judge.

His compassion is real.

That is because he's straight-up been there. He walks, in his words, the walk, and knows, in mine, from whence he talks the talk.

As it happened, our second joint venture was to be this little book, in which his main message, always unfettered and at the forefront of his teaching and ministry, is as clear now as it was then.

Check your pain at the door, clear the way to save your soul. Or, at the very least, live a more soulful life. To many, that's just as important, just as good.

On his suggestion, I myself revisited a few choice memories, a la this book's M.O., came face to bloody face with some evil, powerful achin' at their core. God as I know Him eased it.

That in itself is a colossal miracle – a life-changing change at least. I realize now that P-Low, really, just teaches the righteous way to actually behave – how to represent. For me, he's steady as she goes.

So, I say! You heard it here first, folks, that L.F. Low's *YOUR PAIN IS SHOWING!*, this book – I call it his pain-management manual – is good for absolutely everybody. And I've read it. A lot.

With it, then, in one hand, and the other lifted skyward, have your pain stripped away through a simple – but not without its craggy obstacles – trip down "memory lane."

Daryl Jung
Toronto, Canada
Spring, 2011

Preface/Author's Note

*M*odern science and Christianity, philosophically speaking, draw increasingly closer together with each passing decade.

Through this real and major evolution, a singularly fundamental and contemporary question surfaces: Is science proving the existence of God, or is it God allowing science to find Him?

My money is right on the latter. Just look at what Scriptures have taught all along,

"For with the heart one believes unto righteousness, and with the mouth confession is made unto salvation." (Romans 10:10)

Compare this with the recent discoveries of leading-edge microbiologist Dr. Bruce H. Lipton and his marauding band of quantum physics crusaders at the Stanford University School of Medicine.[1] These guys are real heavyweights.

Lipton has roundly challenged the entire scientific community with the idea that, as he puts it,

"Charles Darwin's dog-eat-dog version of evolution – and biology's central premise that genes control life – is flawed. In more scientific terms, genes are not self-emergent. Simply put, genes cannot turn themselves on or off – they must be triggered into

---

[1] Dr. Bruce Lipton, *The Biology of Belief* (Mountain of Love/Elite Books), 2005, pg. 12.

action by something in the environment, something they call the 'central voice.'"

Sounds borderline totalitarian, no?

Well, no, it really isn't. That central voice is what we Christians call *faith*. Both epigenetic scientists and microbiologists agree that what we humans believe, as well as what we speak, determines how cells work for us or against us.

"Epigenetics" is "control above genetics," which means we are *not* trapped into being a carbon copy of our daddy, or daddy's daddy.

According to their most solid recent findings (exceptionally exciting for me because of my personal background and experiences) we can control, for better or for worse, our destiny.

We can be healed immediately of deadly diseases and emerge victorious over crushing personal problems and life's tough challenges.

This scientific discovery proves that what the Bible has been saying for 1000's of years is not mere religious fantasy, amped up with dogma, but actual physical reality.

Says Lipton, "Limitations… programmed into the subconscious… influence behavior, they can also play a major role in determining our physiology and health… the mind plays a powerful role in controlling the biological systems that keep us alive."[2]

---

[2] Dr. Bruce Lipton, ibid, pg. 166.

Your Pain Is Showing!

Our mind has recording capabilities, with more memory capacity than we know, much like a "super-computer" hard drive, our subconscious can be reprogrammed.

Here's the killer. Hot-shot science doesn't know how to do that. That's the bad news.

Here's the good, most *exciting* news of all: God knows how to reprogram our minds!

Jesus said we will experience the truth, and will then be free.

The Bible teaches that a transformation occurs as we learn to work toward renewal, with God, through our faith,

"And do not be conformed to this world, but be transformed by the renewing of your mind,"
(Romans 12:2a)

That's what YOUR PAIN IS SHOWING! is all about; how we can change ourselves and lead happier *and* healthier lives in an increasingly dangerous, evil world, in the process.

L.F. Low
Zoë Ministries
Colfax, Iowa, USA

Dedication

This book is dedicated to:

All the men and women who have, or will, come to Teen Challenge of the Midlands seeking freedom from the pains of life while searching for the pathway to peaceful living. To you I humbly dedicate this work in hopes that it might make some of your journey easier and more readily understood. It is an honor to serve you as I follow God. Because of you and your desire to live in peace, I have found a renewed importance for my life, for which I will be forever grateful.

The leadership of Teen Challenge, who made this work possible and encouraged me to follow through with it. I thank you for trusting me with the ongoing responsibility of mentoring and helping mold men and women of God into a rational, rejuvenated generation of Christian leadership. Your service, vision for ministry and compassion for students is commendable and unusual in an age of greed, personal political agendas, self-service and path-of-least-resistance ministry.

Introduction

"He who believes in Me, the works that I do he will do also; and greater works he will do." (John 14:12)[3]

As modern Christians, we regularly and steadfastly train our sights on Jesus Christ as the ultimate example of how to live.

We also see in Him the vast potential for whom and what we can become – illuminated for us, all over the New Testament, is the righteous path to realizing that potential.

If we follow that light, keeping our eyes fixed upon Jesus, God grants us the grace to become what He has destined us to be.

Human beings cannot *be* God – very obviously and thankfully – but we can become just as Jesus was while living and walking on earth.

He was greatly charismatic, self-assured and powerful; yet obedient or more accurately, submissive to His Heavenly Father.

---

[3] All Scriptures references from the New King James Version of the Holy Bible unless otherwise noted.

To become like Him, God has given us the abilities, as His children, to accomplish what Jesus did. There is more to it, though, than that.

Astonishingly – according to His explicit words in John 14, verse 12 – Jesus intends for us to accomplish even *greater* things than He!

But as long as we think we can figure out how to conduct our lives on our own, we will not. We will accomplish very little – next to nothing.

Until we break out of our naturally and electronically conditioned, second millennium human methods of thinking – and embrace almighty God's methods – we will not enjoy the absolute freedom He intends for us.

Importantly, we can find this life of perfect peace and unending inner joy in only one way – through unfettered and unequivocal obedience to God and fervent faith in His son Jesus Christ.

But do not despair. Take a deep breath. To do this does *not* automatically result in a stuffy, boring or confining lifestyle, as many casual observers would have us believe.

In fact, the more earnestly we submit to God, the more blessed peace flows over us – and into and back out of us, cleansed – like a giant air purifier.

This translates into a long, clean and sweet life of fulfillment, quietude, confidence and true gratification of living on, and caring for, the earth, as well as our fellow human beings.

We are His most glorious creations.

Your Pain Is Showing!

The fact remains – since Adam and Eve, men and women have desired and tried, as is our nature, to figure out for ourselves how to live the lives God gave us. We couldn't leave well enough alone.

All it took was a cunningly crafted question from a charming and sarcastic snake to lead Eve to conclude that she and Adam were not somehow good enough as they were. They wanted more.

The single lie they believed caused them to cross the one moral line God drew for them, sending them – and consequently the rest of humanity – into guilt, condemnation and shame; leaving us, ultimately, without a Savior.

Not a good situation!

God alone can rectify it, as only God can alter the heart of humankind.

Part of His process allows us the freedom of choice in all matters of life. We haven't any choice but to comprehend and receive this revelation – unless we wise up and *invite* God into our bad situations, He cannot help us.

Our faith in Jesus' work on the cross opens the door to unimaginable strength and blessings, but we must request and cooperate to actually receive it all.

If we do not then open our hearts to the awaiting treasures of a life following Jesus, we will never be able to successfully complete our God-given mission on this earth – not to mention live out our destiny in His company in Heaven.

Gentle reader, as you navigate your way through the following teachings, you may at times deem them a bit clinical in process, with personality-altering and behavior-modification as some sort of psychological goal, or, "desired result."

Nothing could be *further* from the truth.

The primary purpose of this book is to assist readers in understanding why God's children are the way they are – and how we must endeavor to change what we see in ourselves.

It also aims to help Christian and other readers in experiencing profound and positive life changes, and direct them individually toward a deeper and more intimate relationship with God.

Only then may all of humanity change.

This, to boot, is the very, main, numero-uno reason God put His Spirit in us,

> *"...to guide us into all truth...to speak and tell us of things to come."* (John 16:13)

Jesus said in Acts 1, verse 8 that when the Holy Spirit comes upon us, we receive power to be witnesses of His life around the world.

Being a witness to His life means being an "eye witness." We must *experience* His life.

As He goes on to explain, we cannot testify as witnesses if we have only intellectually learned of His life and experiences, because then our testimony is mere hearsay. It's unsubstantiated.

Therefore, we can only qualify as witnesses when we have experienced first-hand – and believe in with all our hearts and souls – what Jesus said, saw, felt, heard, experienced.

We can't bear witness to the fact that God raises the dead unless we have been a vessel through whom He *has* raised the dead.

Nor do we qualify as witnesses that God is redeeming sinners unless we have experienced personal redemption, and become His beacon that shines only to lead other people to Him.

Everything God did in Scripture, He is still doing today. Yes, He is.

I learned early in my walk with Jesus to listen, to obey the *voice* of the Holy Spirit. Because of staunch obedience to Him, I experience His hands working through me – and for me – every time I turn around.

I have seen two people revived from being dead, instant healings of cancer and lupus, and the conversion of many hundreds of folks to the great Kingdom of God in my one-on-one ministry encounters with them.

I marvel still at the amazing, real miracle that occurred directly to my benefit, wherein, on a Mexico missions trip, our incredulous group passed out hundreds of pairs of brand new shoes to the impoverished of the area.

Our van had originally contained just 20!

Every day I witness God accomplishing what science, medicine and psychology have never done – instantly and permanently heal years of emotional trauma and physical pain through obedience to His very voice, His actual voice.

This, too, has always been a part of God's promises for those who believe,

"But God has chosen the foolish things of the world to put to shame the wise, and God has chosen the weak things of the world to put to shame the things which are mighty;" (1Corinthians 1:27)

Remember, though, our Lord *God* is the miracle-worker, not us. He desires to have His power flowing *through* us. Of that we can be certain.

This happens when we get humble enough to recognize that we lack the wherewithal to do anything for Him on our own power,

"…for without Me you can do nothing."
(John 15:3b)

It is a big mistake, it should be noted, to live just *for* God. It clears the way for a whole lot of thorny frustration, confusion and eventual defeat.

Rather, we are able to live *out of* God by abiding in Him, and grow and prosper, like an ecstatic and radiant rose rising out of fresh, fertile soil, in our relationship with Him.

Doing so produces, without fail, the sweet fruit of righteousness. This is living proof of God working through us.

I pray this book increases understanding of what it means to live out of God.

Your Pain Is Showing!

I believe that our journey to God commences when we learn to communicate, organically, our personal issues to Him – those often deep-seeded fears and dark memories that haunt us and stand between us and the bright, abundant life He promises.

Do you fully grasp that last paragraph? If you don't, the rest of this book won't make much sense.

Therefore, I will repeat it; just in case – experiencing God begins when we take steps to directly communicate our personal issues to Him, vocally and daily.

If we don't start there, we don't start at all.

The name of the subsequent wonderful process to glorious victory and pure freedom is Christianity – humankind walking in close harmony and fellowship with God, as Jesus did during His time on earth.

Until we begin to truly *listen* to – as well as obey – the voice of the amazing Holy Spirit, we are doomed to live with stark inner discord and debilitating fear.

This prevents us, the hobbyist Christians and the rest of the secular world from seeing the spiritual riches, divinely inspired behavior and pure paradigms contained within *every one* of us.

We just must join forces with God.

In Jesus Christ, there is always hope.

If we put all the Scriptures (and their instructions) invoked here in this book into practice, as we carefully navigate through life on this wild and wooly planet we can complete the process. Change our lives.

It is then, Christians, that the world sees in us – through *you* – how great our God is!

PART I
ATTITUDE

Chapter One
Attitude Is A Big Deal

*Y*ou're at the local mall.

After late church and a lovely lunch on a bright, shiny spring Sunday, you stroll along peacefully with your family, enjoying quite the refreshing ice cream.

Life is good.

Your eyes happily, naturally, take in the bustling surroundings, and you are feeling kindly, after some fine fellowship, toward all of it – from the delighted squeals of young children to the knowing, contented glances of elderly couples.

Your gaze meanders further, comes briefly to rest on a tattooed, pierced, leathered, skin-headed kid displaying racist hate gang colors.

Mild fear immediately overtakes you, but you manage a smile, knowing that Jesus would have us love even the hurting, misguided souls who deal with pain, hate and anguish with anger, violence and intimidation.

Your Pain Is Showing!

"What the *@#%&$!* are you smiling at?" he scowls bitterly. "You were givin' me some kinda freakin' attitude, church man!"

You're startled, afraid, concerned for your family's safety. You feel cornered, exposed, attacked – any negative emotion that causes you to wish very dearly you were anywhere else, facing *anyone* else.

"No I wasn't! What attitude?" you stammer, too frightened to formulate words even remotely close to what Jesus would have uttered.

"I don't have an attitude!"

Oh yes, you do.

* * *

We all do; even born again believers. We hear about it hundreds of times a day, in every kind of situation – attitude, attitude, *attitude*.

Just repeating it three times has become an American slogan in its own right.

What is attitude – or an attitude – for that matter? Does it matter so much to understand our attitudes? How do they affect us and the other important people in our lives?

Are they hurting people or lives on any level, and if so, which ones, and on what level?

What *is* the big deal, anyway?

Geeks like Daniel Webster are more often than not helpful in these situations, and true to form, they break down the definition of "attitude" concisely into four general types.

An attitude is first a "mental position," taken for situations dealing with facts or decision-making. Attitude can also be the actual physical positioning of the body that indicates mood or state of mind.

Attitude is as well a manner of behavior, emotion or thinking that betrays opinion; and finally, an attitude can be the opinion itself, a disposition or a "mental set."

Others think of attitude as a "pattern" of thinking, a "specific" opinion, a developed thinking "habit" or point of view based on the thought and experience that has occurred and accumulated throughout life.

For 50 plus years I battled to control my own attitude, and in the past 20 years I have actively helped other people change theirs.

That said, my informed, but ever-humble adjustment to the contemporary definition is: Our attitude is the physical expression, or our natural presentation, of what life *feels* like – and its *source* is how *we feel* about our lives.

I embrace this definition because it has proven to be 100 per cent accurate over my entire time dealing with suffering folks from all ethnicities, occupations and lifestyles who have come to me for help.

It has also been essential in helping me change my own, formerly destructive (self-, and otherwise) attitudes – which held me back physically, emotionally and spiritually.

Today I espouse nothing but very healthy, positive and joyous attitudes, which propel me through the beautiful daily grind of guiding troubled folks to the peace of Jesus.

In most cases, attitude is what makes life easy – or tough – for people. Mostly, though, it's tough. Before anything else, they have to realize that a right attitude can open many doors.

Inappropriate attitudes close the same ones.

I try to guide them to the old adage that their *attitudes,* not *aptitudes,* control their *altitude.*

Well-known Christian author and teacher, Pastor Charles Swindoll, has this to say of it:

"The longer I live, the more I realize the impact of attitude on life. Attitude, to me, is more important than facts.

"It is more important than the past, than education, than money, than circumstances, than failures, than successes, than what other people think, say, or *do*. It is more important than appearance, skill or giftedness.

"We cannot change the fact that people will act in a certain way. We cannot change the inevitable. The only thing we can do is play on the one string we have, and that is our attitude... I am convinced that life is 10 per cent what happens and 90 per cent how I react to it. And so it is with you. We are in charge of our attitudes."[4]

In other words, attitude is something we absolutely must understand and learn to adjust – in

---

[4] Charles Swindoll, *Great Attitudes* (Thomas Nelson) 2006; also www.bigeye.com/attitude.htm.

order to fly with metaphorical eagles, soaring far above the toughest battles and through the most raging storms of life.

In the face of such adversities, we wonder if it's even possible to change our attitudes.

If we fully understand the cause of the attitudes that need changing, and seek the right type of help necessary to do so, the answer is a resounding,

"Yes!"

Chapter Two
Attitude Vs. Aptitude

*W*e can glide as high as we may desire, succeed extravagantly as we wish and live the "good life" – as long as our attitude allows.

Our attitudes will in fact either propel us to great accomplishments or drag us down into a pitiful pit of despair and destruction.

This is why it is imperative, to live the abundant life Jesus intends for us, to better understand how to monitor, manipulate, and then mold more serviceable new attitudes.

Aptitude, on the other hand, is the sum of our natural and continually developing – or learned – abilities designed by God and nature for specific human purposes.

The more we learn, the more complete – and useful and fun! – our aptitudes become. That should go without saying.

I like to say that aptitude is what we are *apt-to-do* – or what we have learned to do. It is the easier of the two A-words to deal with, because instinct, along with the repetition of training, turns actions into second nature.

This allows us to respond to and act on most natural impulses of life without thinking about it much. They are automatic.

We spend great fortunes, then, developing higher aptitude through self-improvement programs, adult education classes and endless practice of various newly acquired skills.

Alas, after spending a bundle and burning up our biographies chasing our aptitudes for success, many of us still fail to live our dreams or meet our full potential because we are not adept at identifying or changing our attitudes.

Rarely do we give our attitudes much of a thought, even if they are destroying our potential and holding us back from achieving the promised fulfillment of living *out of* God.

Attitude, consequently, directly affects our tolerance, or level of patience – how much stress and agitation we can endure at the hands of others before we snap. Job and Jesus had the most ever.

We have established that the source of attitude is our feelings, but the source of what we feel is only what we subconsciously believe to be true about ourselves, real or otherwise.

This belief, our interpretation, has been stored in our memories. Sadly to say, it is seldom, if ever, the actual truth.

Programmed right into what I call our "super-computer," though, are subconscious interpretations of experiences that continually mix and mesh with our learning, knowledge and memory.

God knows computers, rest assured.

Then it all fuses together, creating the feelings that raise or lower tolerance levels, develop or change our attitudes and color the lenses through which we see the world – our paradigms (see Chapter 11, page 77).

All of this subconscious activity drives us toward our future. To change our paradigms and tolerance levels, along with our attitudes, we must change the raw interpretations of all our experiences – or re-program our super-computers.

We do this by wholeheartedly communicating to God what we believe about ourselves and let Him decide on its validity.

People who come to me are shocked at how readily He refutes the "truth" of their version of events that adversely affected them.

This reinterpretation of memories leaves us with a positive feeling. This then morphs into the positive attitude necessary to stave off the ceaseless bombardment of the negative aspects of living in an increasingly treacherous world.

Once we reprogram our subconscious with God's perfect truth, paradigms automatically restructure and tolerance naturally increases.

That's about it in a nutshell.

Easy. Right?

On the surface, you may well question this logic, thinking that changing the results of our past is impossible.

Therefore the world generally subscribes to such adages as, "No use crying over spilt milk," or, "Once an addict always an addict."

Psychologists realize this is patently false, but have for decades still tried unsuccessfully to change the results of our past.

Some mad radicals have even gone to the extreme of destroying patients' (read victims) minds altogether through irresponsible abuse of – and experimentation with – medications, frontal lobotomy or electroshock treatments.

The Bible, however, says,

"With men this is impossible, but with God all things are possible." (Matthew 19:26)

This is the primary reason Jesus came to earth – to teach us that reality by helping us renew our minds through the reprogramming of our subconscious,

"And be not conformed to the pattern of this world but be transformed by the renewing of your mind. (Romans 12:2a)

We have established that the emotional pain we inflict on ourselves comes from subconsciously recalling misinterpreted experiences.

This inevitably, invariably results in a condition we refer to as a "broken" heart.

Your Pain Is Showing!

Jesus came to heal the broken-hearted,

"The Spirit of the Lord God is upon Me, because the Lord has anointed Me to preach good tidings to the poor; He has sent Me to heal the brokenhearted…"
(Isaiah 61:1a; Luke 4:18a)

Jesus also said,

"I am the way, the truth and the life."
(John 14:6a)

He is saying that without a way to truth, there *is* no life. It is essential that we have a consistent source of perfect truth available to us, in order to succeed living the life of inner peace humankind has always sought – and largely failed to achieve.

Therefore, He said,

"If you abide in My Word, you are My disciples indeed. And you shall know the truth and the truth shall make you free." (John 8:31, 32)

To understand properly how these verses actually bring freedom to our lives, we need to grasp why and how the device God gave us to perceive the world, our unbelievable brain,[5] subconsciously interprets our every experience.

This process is the brain's only method of protecting itself – and all of the body – and is necessary for self-preservation *before* a person has leapt onto the bandwagon of Jesus.

The process treats every life experience we have as philosopher's stones in the foundation of self-protection and preservation.

All that our receptors (sight, touch, taste, smell and hearing) receive (a mind-boggling amount of information, no pun intended) is registered in our subconscious as memory.

First and foremost in our brain, as it performs this protective function of interpretation, is the fundamental question of what a particular experience makes us feel about ourselves.

This helps explain our natural instinctual response when initially encountering someone who is angry or upset. Typically, we throw up our hands, shrug our shoulders, and ask,

"Why me? What did *I* do?"

When people inside our immediate circles become visibly upset or create real drama as a public spectacle, it makes us uncomfortable.

More often than not, in our naturally self-absorbed attempt to protect and perfect ourselves, we credit

---

[5] When I speak of the natural mind, human brain, or the natural state I refer to concepts with no connection to God, held by those who never learned how to control their mind's natural self-protective process.

ourselves as the cause of their suffering and assume blame for it.

We assume their misery must be our fault rather than knowing the facts.

We can, and often do, assume that their response is an attack on us, not considering that they may be suffering from something quite apart – and likely more significant – from ourselves. Surprise, surprise!

This is one of the many reasons why the majority of our interpretations end up being false; resulting in our ridiculous, but very real, recordings of *lies* for these particular events.

This automatic function of our brains started while developing in the womb. All experience (good, bad, transcendent), is stored in our subconscious mind.

Because this part of our brain contains our feelings and experiences – not raw data per se – I also refer, throughout this book, to the super-computer as our "experiential" memory.

Our brain never forgets anything unless a physical injury destroys memory. This refers not to our cognitive ability to absorb and recall information, but to the brain's ability to retain it and make use of it subconsciously.

Some memories we may well like to forget. Some, we might think we have put behind us. The reason we can't shake them permanently is, they are vital information, necessary to the body's natural self-protection program.

On the other side of this coin – the shiny side – the Lord also utilizes the entirety of information in our memories to help us grow, both emotionally and spiritually.

Things we have tried to forget often leap to the forefront of our minds and we tend to quickly trivialize, if not outright dismiss them with, "Where did *that* come from?!"

These odd moments are called flashbacks, 1960s implications notwithstanding. In reality they are, very likely, God's attempt to alert us to past situations He can help us resolve.

Our industrious super-computers compare every experience of every single day to all past experiences stored in memory as it searches for similar situations that once hurt us.

This is the first of two steps that our minds automatically employ to protect our bodies. Smashing our thumbs with a hammer poses a good example of the brain's defense system.

The next time we pick up a hammer and nail, our brains automatically remind us of the results of last time. We remember the pain.

That next time, we might resort to holding the nail with a pair of pliers because our brain is screaming at us, "Doh! Uh, duh! Don't *do* it! You're gonna hurt yourself – again – dummy. Don't you remember last time?"

The thumb sure does! It's reacting now to an event that happened a while ago. The brain determines that a current experience is similar to another, the pain of past occurrences felt today – a bona fide déjà vu moment.

Your Pain Is Showing!

We rarely – if ever – actually see the past painful experience (memory "picture") in our mind's eye. We do, though, feel its pain repeatedly as the key-points of the current situation trigger the old experience.

This is the mind's way of shielding the body from physical injury, the heart from emotional damage, itself from psychic harm.

And it all shakes down in nanoseconds, and subconsciously. Science has proven that, as much as 98 per cent of all we say and do is the product of this subconscious process.[6]

The subconscious, the ol' super-computer, works in the present and is reflexive in nature, not controlled by thought or reason.

When we have an original experience that doesn't trigger anything in the subconscious memory, our brain passes that information along to yet another phase of our natural protection mechanism – intellect.

In this stage we intellectually, or rationally, analyze the immediate flow of fact and critical details and compare them to what's already stored in our cognitive database.

This is where we make and perform our art, do our good work, recognize responsibilities and make decisions about our lives.

As this cognitive process is taking place, we also, quite subconsciously, tend to interpret any unfamiliar

---

[6] Dr Bruce Lipton, *The Biology Of Belief* (Elite Books) 2005, pg. 133.

experience based on how it makes us feel about ourselves.

Once interpreted, the entire incident, along with its corresponding emotions, becomes a permanent part of our experiential memory or subconscious database. It remains part of us.

For most of my life, I hated playing board games, cards or anything where there was any chance whatsoever of my losing – triggering my anger.

I had a bitter, angry attitude, was rotten with negative energy, with no patience for anyone or anything. My attitude forced me to be pathologically careful. It seemed everyone was out to get me.

My lack of patience kept me on a jagged edge, which compelled me to defend myself viciously and unnecessarily against everything and everybody. My neck was always sore from looking over my shoulder.

I was what we now call paranoid. Paranoia strikes deep. Into your life it will creep.

I never understood why I was always angry until the day I asked God to show me the origin of my rage. He showed me the memory of an experience I had forgotten I even had, as a nine-year-old boy.

I always dreamed of staying home from school and working with my dad, as most kids will do from time to time.

That special day finally arrived and there I was, blissfully working cattle alongside my dad and uncle. As they labored to wean, cut and inject terrified calves, I ran the sorting gate.

Then a freaked-out cow, distraught at the sound of her bleating calf, charged the gate. Rather than stand firm and do the job, I let go of it and headed for the proverbial hills.

As earnest as I was, I obviously had little success doing an as effective job as the adults. A child has no way of keeping up with men – a fact well known by all but the boy himself.

At any rate, what I did was, inevitably, blatantly wrong, which intensified my uncle's disappointment at my making more work for the men.

The moment I saw that almost pained look on his face, I believed that no matter what or how I tried I would *never* be able to make up for my folly, nor be good – at anything, *ever*.

Oh, how inadequate this made me feel!

I subconsciously held this false belief and the ensuing negative emotion until I was 50.

That's a lot of wasted time and energy.

Up to this time, I had never been able to consciously see, understand or acknowledge that inadequacy was what I was actually feeling.

Every single time any experience would trigger this dark subconscious memory, rage and resentment would muscle right in, Guido-like, to keep me from identifying it.

Suddenly, as I so vividly experienced that four-decade-old memory, it became crystal clear to me that my anger was indeed rooted in my feelings of inadequacy. Simple as that.

Never in my life had I consciously revisited this particular memory. I now know, though, that I'd been feeling its pain every time an event overwhelmed me or I faced failing at anything I set out to do.

In my attempts over the years to free myself from my constant, nagging rage and the consequent agonizing bouts of depression, I memorized large sections of Scripture.

Like many people, I thought the good-old reliable Holy Bible, fairly bursting with its unfathomable wisdom, would miraculously and permanently divest me of my sinful responses.

The more I studied and memorized, the more frustrated I became. My anger not only continued, but it picked up gale force over time like a category-four hurricane.

I became a very active alcoholic and came as close to committing suicide as a man can get without actually pulling the trigger of the gun he has pointing directly into his mouth.

I dearly fear, as well, that anyone's own efforts toward artificial self-improvement and enlightenment will not work any better than mine did, because pain is not stored in the intellect, or cognitive memory.

Our pain is felt in the heart and stored in the subconscious memory.

My thoughts and feelings imploded and spiraled downward into a murky sinkhole of despair, and I became as frightful, frantic and frustrated as I had ever been. I was at the end of my tether.

This, in turn, put the final touches on the imminent ruin of my attitude, the trashing of my health and near obliteration of my soul.

Then, suddenly, after asking God why I could not control my anger or my agony, I had an epiphany. I was able to see the original memory as it really was!

When I verbally blurted out to the Lord I felt inadequate, He spoke right to me, saying,

"I didn't make you inadequate. I never make anything inadequate. Everything that I create has a purpose and so do you. When you find your purpose you will see that you are more than adequate."

As I spoke – *aloud* – and sensed what the Lord was saying to me, all the lethal toxins of inadequacy, rage and bitterness drained out.

I have since been free of their effects.[7]

Receiving the Lord's own words of truth profoundly and irrevocably changed what I believed about myself.

My inappropriate, unmanageable attitude instantly transformed from one of a non-trusting, hateful, protect-only-me mind-set to a genuine *joie de vivre*-type joy of living vibe and a loving desire to help other people who currently hurt as much as I had.

After that heavy experience with God, I began to have infinitely more patience with outside forces, myself and others.

---

[7] To read the entire account of this story and understand more fully how God heals our emotional wounds, why we must speak audibly to the Lord what He speaks to us, and why seeing the memory is so important, read the author's previous book, Genuine Christianity, published by American Book Publishing Co., available at Amazon.com, www.LarryLow.com and www.genuinechristianity.org

Now I handle situations that once drove me to fits and spasms of wrath and rancor with humor, calm and reason.

Don't forget that how we inwardly feel about ourselves drives or derails our attitudes and our capacity for compassion for others.

Our intellect is where we *think,* create and do our reasoning. Reflection/thinking is the mind's ultimate coping mechanism.

When confronted with stark pangs of past emotional pain, we immediately begin – *again* – thinking about and relating to the inevitable, immediately ensuing, *need.*

I thank God for intellect, as it told me that ending my life was not the solution to the deadly dilemma facing me.

Over time, the initial, gouging thrust of the pain subsides, or maybe even ends, making us think we have dealt with the issue.

However, as has been discussed, the pain confounds and controls, and tortures, us from our subconscious/experiential memory, which is where we dwell most of the time.

Our experiences and their interpretations (right or wrong, truth or lies) are stored in the subconscious. The conscious mind, or the intellect, is where facts are stored.

With that in mind, it is crucial to examine *how* to receive the truth that has the power to change the results of our past, improve our possibilities for the future – and make us *free.*

* * *

We shall also, then, *know* the truth.

The English word "know" translates from the Greek as any, or all of, "knowledge gained by experience" – which can be random, is often inadvertent and largely out of our control.

Experience with God, however, can and should be initiated by us as we turn toward Him to deal with our inner pain and emotional demons.

It doesn't refer to information or concepts programmed into our minds through our own pre-directed efforts. This is cognitive learning.

Jesus said that we will *experience* the truth and it shall make us free,

"However, when He, the Spirit of truth, has come, He will guide you into all truth; for He will not speak on His own authority, but whatever He hears He will speak; and He will tell you things to come."
(John 16:13)

Freedom comes when He speaks the truth directly to the madness of our misguided methods – and consequent misinterpretation of experience – or the lies that so harm us.

Jesus' truth frees us from the lie, though, *not* our sin. That's already done. He dealt with our sin as we came to His cross to be born again.

According to Scripture, those who actively communicate with Him walk in truth,

"No one who abides in Him [who lives and remains in communion with and in obedience to Him – deliberately, knowingly, and habitually] commits (practices) sin..." (1John 3:6 Amplified Version)

We call this *abiding* in God, and when we abide in Him, we cannot sin.

In Jesus there is no sin.

The kind of sinning that leads to eternal separation is intentionally – and with malice – breaking God's most sacred laws, or spitting in His face.

As we communicate with Him, we are in contact with sweet, perfect, irrefutable truth, and therefore unlikely to disobey willfully.

Chapter Three
Existence And Enlightenment

*O*ur feelings are the nerve-endings of our souls.

Attitude and our overall tolerance levels indicate the health of our souls.

That same health, positive or negative, is visible to others no matter how well we think we hide it. Most of us don't win Oscars.

Our attitude and tolerance is a compilation of all the emotions and experiences we have ever had throughout our life.

We also express, every minute of our lives, those emotions generating from our heart and soul.

The Bible often uses the terms "soul" and "heart" for both our subconscious memories and our conscious, intellectual process.

All we have experienced and learned determines our will, with its firm stronghold within our soul.

Our experiences make us who we are and who we will later become. It is in them that the crucial changes necessary for spiritual and emotional healing and renewal must happen,

> *"Therefore lay aside all filthiness and overflow of wickedness, and receive with meekness the implanted word, which is able to save your souls."* (James 1:21),

and

> *"And do not be conformed to this world, but be transformed by the renewing of your mind,"* (Romans 12:2a)

Almost anyone can control his or her outward physical presentation for a short period.

But given enough time, whether a minute or a millennium, what we truly feel about life, in our heart of hearts, will eventually rear its ugly head – usually when we least expect it.

When we find ourselves pushed beyond our ability to cope, or to "fake it 'til you make it," our world comes crashing down like a Charlie chopper and we plummet into despair.

Times like these cause some Christians to question even the presence of God in their lives, which robs us of hope, faith and thus the sweet peace Jesus promises so solemnly.

When this happens our demeanor changes to reflect the way we feel inside. It is not a pretty picture. We look desperate and mad.

Your Pain Is Showing!

For the majority of us, it results in an attitude others do not, to put it mildly, enjoy being around. It frightens and disturbs them.

In cases like this we hurt ourselves, loved ones, associates and – the most staggering loss of all – our chances of finding peace in Jesus.

It is important to understand that the pain of subconsciously recalling the unpleasant and life-shattering events of our past incites and urges on this negative behavior.

The burning question becomes, "How on earth do I change the *effects* of my past?"

Over the past 130 (and change) years, the world's most distinguished, and well-meaning, medical minds have gamely attempted to change attitudes and have failed miserably and consistently.

Our penal system is a white elephant of an example of a failed concept that attempts to change people's ways through incarceration as "punishment." That's a good one.

Convicts come out of incarceration with attitudes dictated by fellow criminals and gang rule and their other ungodly penitentiary experiences.

The increasingly low success rate of secular crime/violence/drug/alcohol rehabilitation programs is yet another example of society's failure to change acquired behavior by cognitive methods.

God has given us the innate and incredible ability to manipulate our amazing bodies as well as our magnificent minds – cognitive thinking ability and physical acumen alike.

However, it is only with God's assistance that we can ever expect significant and lasting changes from within. The subconscious is the area that God has reserved for Himself.

No person alive can change another person's subconscious. Hypnosis might attempt it, but the positive results are vastly questionable.

Doctors who practice hypnosis agree that they are unable to make anyone do anything that goes against their will – never mind the barking chickens.

Even God Himself can't change us unless we choose to allow His Word's knowledge in.

Furthermore, blaming others for the way we behave is an out-right cop-out. The "devil made me do it" days are over, my friends.

Real-deal Christians are responsible for their own feelings because they have instant access to the truth. They must, and do, adhere to it.

Most church leaders believe mortal sin to be the fundamental cause of a Christian's emotional pains, physical addictions, improper behavior and poor attitudes. Not conversely.

Their natural, if ill-considered, conclusion is that if we just quit sinning, our attitude will change. They regard addiction, for example, as a sin, an evil choice, something shameful.

All an alcoholic need do, in their mind, is cease and desist to so blatantly commit that sin of drunkenness and his or her dependence on drink will miraculously disappear.

Most of us have heard, at some time in our lives, "just get over it," "shake it off," "grow up," "gut it out" or "be a man."

This response comes from the speaker's self-righteous misapprehension that sneers,

"Once I present you with a better pattern of behavior, or guilt you out enough about your improper conduct, you'll be able to just adjust your actions to meet *my* standards."

Well, when we tried to get over it, or gut it out, did it ever work? Even once?

When we confess sin, does it keep us from doing it again, knowing, as we do, that God has and would again forgive and cleanse us?

Of course it doesn't.

Hence, a large majority of Christians are confused, frustrated, and self-defeated by the lie that they are not good enough for God to love and protect them as much as others who *seem* to have it all "together."

There is yet another school of incorrect thought among believers which claims that because one is *newly* Christian, they should be immediately and automatically exempt from any more bad feelings or negative attitudes.

Among the many who believe this, some blame the devil himself for causing their inner pain and assume they are in need of deliverance from his evil.

However, what we need, according to Romans 12, verses 1 and 2, is a transformation caused by the renewing of our mind with truth, not deliverance,

> *"I beseech you therefore, brethren, by the mercies of God, that you present your bodies a living sacrifice, holy and acceptable to God, which is your reasonable service. And do not be conformed to this world, but be transformed by the renewing of your mind, that you may prove what is that good and acceptable and perfect will of God."*

That we overreact and behave atrociously in many situations is pudding proof – pain drives us, not vice versa. In a mental arm-wrestle, pain wins hands down.

Our inner pain causes us to be "short" (impatient and disrespectful) with people we love and behave like someone other than who we are. Negative attitudes and intolerance are pain-motivated behavior.

The sinful behavior of the Christian is not the cause of his or her pain. Not at all. Their pain is the cause of their sinful behavior! The sociopathic behavior is propelled by painful feelings and angry mind-set to begin with.

It is, in three words, a vicious circle.

If we have a hurtful or hateful attitude, we are allowing our pain to manipulate us.

We make that choice on our own. At that point, some ask, "Can't God just change me?"

The answer is simple, not to mention self-evident. He will not violate our free will. God can release us from our pain, but we must *invite* Him to do so. *And* be willing pupils.

This critical "face-to-face" communication, necessary to receive the essential inner healing and build our faith, is the expression of faith, and is the most effective means to forging a profound, intimate relationship with Him.

Therefore, without *verbal* communication, with our lips and tongues and teeth and vocal chords, none of this occurs. It is through our mouths that we express our ideas, our will, our joy and fear, as well as our faith in God.

If we are not verbally communicating with God, we are not expressing our faith in Him.

Faith levels the playing field when it comes to working with, and learning from God.

The laws of faith restrain Him, but our expression of faith in Him frees Him to pour out on us the same blessings He did for the saints and patriarchs who came before us, including Jesus himself.

In our dealings with other people, no relationship may evolve without the necessary communication.

God is no different.

Absolutely everything He's ever done – from the beginning of time until this very moment – He has done it expressly to guarantee an intimate relationship with us. He expects us to communicate.

We must open our mouths. Speak to Him!

Achieving liberation from the pain and sorrow of our dark pasts allows and roundly encourages us to behave in fresh, renewed, more acceptable and enlightened ways. We respond, walk softly, smile.

Our attitude subsequently modifies, our tolerance intensifies, and we are ready and able to learn and apply godly principles to succeed in the life He has given us.

Now, the next logical query remains: How, then, does God change our feelings in order to help us modify our attitudes?

Chapter Four
Spiritual Or Psychological?

"*T*hat's the spirit!"

How many times have we heard or said those words – nine times out of 10, I'll bet, sincerely and enthusiastically?

Rightly so. There are innumerable aspects of the spirit about which to be enthusiastic.

Definition-ologists lay out the word "spirit" as the element – or singular ability – in people by which they perceive, reflect, feel, desire, purpose, aim – seems to cover it all!

To perceive is to attain awareness through the senses, or the feelings. Ergo, in terms of the human experience God has given us, spirit is more or less everything. It drives and inspires all we do.

Some Bible translations use "attitude" in place of "spirit," and they are interchangeable in Ephesians 4, verses 23 and 24,

"But you have not so learned Christ, if indeed you have heard Him and have been taught by Him, as the truth is in Jesus: that you put off, concerning your former conduct, the old man which grows corrupt according to the deceitful lusts, and be renewed in the spirit of your mind, and that you put on the new man which was created according to God, in true righteousness and holiness."
(Ephesians 4:20-24)

In order to understand fully the process of changing our attitudes, it is imperative to recognize that this Scripture identifies the area of the soul that produces our emotions as the spirit, or attitude, of our minds.

Working with God to change our attitudes very much involves the arduous business of conceiving of and putting on the "new man," according to God's specifications and in true righteousness and holiness.

Look at Ephesians 4, verses 17 through 19, where the Holy Spirit encourages us to be *not* as we were,

"This I say, therefore, and testify in the Lord, that you should no longer walk as the rest of the Gentiles walk, in the futility of their mind, having their understanding darkened, being alienated from the life of God, because of the ignorance that is in them, because of the blindness of their heart; who, being past

feeling, have given themselves over to lewdness, to work all uncleanness with greediness."

We're not to flounder in the futility of our "lost" minds, alienate God with our ignorance or possess blind, apathetic hearts, taking us past feeling and giving us over to dishonesty, greed, unseemliness and selfishness.

To be beyond feeling results in attempts to cope with issues we face on our own, rather than casting them onto the Lord, running from life's hurts and blaming others for "making" us feel things we do not want to feel.

God instructed us through Apostle Peter how to handle these struggles when he said,

"Therefore humble yourselves under the mighty hand of God, that He may exalt you in due time, casting all your care upon Him, for He cares for you."
(1Peter 5:6, 7)

We might refuse to admit we have any bad feelings at all, for fear that some might judge the admission a confession of guilt or as some sort of weakness or character flaw.

As has been stated, emotions are the soul's nerve endings. They warn us, siren-like, of the pain-inducing lies that strike like public transit workers in our heart, and work constantly to separate us from each other – and, many times, from God Himself.

The key to transformation is *hearing* God speak the truth that is Jesus. As we allow Him to fortify us, we shed the hoary, coarse and scaly skin that is the "old man" or woman to unveil the smooth, unblemished attitudes of our new, enlightened minds.

No other process can achieve this change. The voice of God, speaking to our issues and teaching us how to respond, is the only power capable of transforming us into the complete persons He originally created us to be.

To be born-again proves you have heard Christ (Ephesians 4:20, 21); for no one can be born-again without hearing from God,

"No one can come to Me unless the Father who sent Me draws him;" (John 6:44a)

The soul, or what I call the spirit of the mind, is where all that we believe cognitively and know experientially come together.

This union forms feelings as it develops attitudes on life generally and us specifically.

Many places in Scripture actually refer to the soul as the heart, evident in the Greek use of their word for heart, "kardia."[8]

The new interpreter's commentary's definition[9] expands on the implications of the switch,

---

[8] Strong's Dictionary vocabulary helps reference number 2588.

[9] *The Hebrew-Greek Key Study Bible* published by AMG Publishers, Chattanooga, TN 37422. Compiled and edited by Spiros Zodhiates, Th.D.

"Scriptures attribute to the heart thoughts, reasoning, understanding, judgment, design, affection, love, hatred, fear, joy, sorrow, and anger since these things can actually affect a man's physical heart… thoughts and emotions affect blood pressure. Therefore, heart is used for mind in general."

As we've discovered, medical minds have never been able to affect a permanent change in attitude. It's because psychiatry and psychology still insist on only approaching the problem from the outside, working – like ants up a hill – in.

After 50 or so years of competent effort and earnest trial and error, our best secular substance addiction, severe mental pathology and criminal rehabilitation efforts – the programs, punishments and pressures – have failed for the same reason, and for all to plainly see.

The way to have control of our feelings is to make a significant change from the inside – or, namely, from our hearts out.

Jesus' truth first must explode within our souls, then the power of Jesus' peace allows us to transform into beautiful, bran-spankin' new beings, ready to calmly receive life's calamities.

The teachings presented here refer often to how we present our physical countenance to our environment, compared with what God has in mind when we put on the "new man" – who is new inside and out; strong, self-possessed, devout.

Born again believers have an aura, a glow about them that won't be denied.

Some might call this "transcendence.' The Bible calls it "transformation."

The next step is to examine it, and look at how to apply this transformational process to developing new attitudes, increased tolerance and proper paradigms.

Chapter Five
Undergoing Metamorphosis

Change is good. God endorses it.

Every wonder of, and in, His amazing, infinite creation – such as, to name a few, the weather, seasons, the minds, bodies, moods, interests, weight and hairlines of humans – changes.

God's world is in a constant state of flux.

As Christians, it can become necessary to change our attitudes, paradigms and behavior in order to maintain an even keel on our trip through life, leading to Jesus' side in Heaven,

"And do not be conformed to this world but be transformed by the renewing of your mind that you may prove what is that good and acceptable and perfect will of God." (Romans 12: 1-2)

Metamorphosis is the process wherein an absolute fundamental restructuring takes place inside the organism, resulting in dramatic and permanent change of existence.

The process is internal, but the profound aesthetic and functional change is evident only externally. We're talkin' major modification.

The most evident and easily identifiable lepidopterological example of all of this is the butterfly. A plumpish, ugly caterpillar spins a cocoon around itself, dies, and emerges a delicate, breathtakingly beautiful new creature.

The glorious final product is the stellar opposite of its original gross form.

Where the caterpillar was unable to get off the ground, the butterfly is incapable, or at least loathsome, of staying there.

The original creature is slow, creepy, inelegant and cumbersome. What comes from it is a transformed, and therefore transcendent, living miracle – sweetly winged, graceful and majestic.

Christians constantly try to undergo and complete this transformation that God desires from the "outside in," by erroneously thinking we might eventually read, learn, and memorize enough Bible to put that change into effect.

What we fail to understand is that reading and memorization change only our cognitive memory and our intellect. Very rarely will it alter experiential memory, or subconscious.

Reading may occasionally help, but on its own, it will not produce the inner change we need, because the problems, or the lies, exist only in the subconscious memory.

God dwells inside Christians because,

"...the Spirit of truth, whom the world cannot receive, because it neither sees Him nor knows Him; but you know Him, for He dwells with you and will be in you." (John 14:17)

When He speaks to our pain, or these lies, His Word produces a transformation *inside* us, which then changes our presentation.

Only God can speak to our subconscious memory. That is why psychology has never been able to take away the pain of anyone's out-of-sync personal life.

All input from the outside is intellectual data, while all input from within is via the Holy Spirit, and affects the subconscious super computer as well as our conscious, and contentious, intellect.

I am not at all against reading and memorizing scripture, by any means. I do a great deal of it myself. Doing it gives the Holy Spirit within us more raw clay to sculpt. Plus, it inspires and instructs.

Reading the Bible *feeds* our spirit and soul. Beyond that, we must hear and receive the truth from the One who *is* Truth in order to transform internally.

However, trying to change the inner person by reading and memorizing data from the outside in is like taping paper wings on a caterpillar to make it fly.

Only God can take a clumsy, unsightly caterpillar and implement such a miraculous and stunning transformation.

Likewise, only God can address, from the center of our very complex mechanism, the thoughts and memories within our subconscious.

When He does, lies believed yesterday give way today to His update of the truth.

Chapter Six
Communicating With God

*C*ontrolling and deleting the deadly lies we believed about ourselves yesterday – and then inserting God's ideal, illuminating truth today – is impossible until we make communicating effectively with Him second nature.

Many Christians, who have worshiped and prayed silently in their own way for umpteen years, naturally assume they have been talking to God.

Unfortunately, when you get into their issues of life, the truth is, their assumption is *all* they know.

You can tell when you look at the fruit and/or pain of their lives.

Many don't realize we can take this blessing to dizzying new heights, making the most of our walk with God in the process. We might assume we know how to talk to Him, but there are myriad believers who absolutely do not.

To rectify that, I center my entire ministry on helping people seek, find – and hear – the voice of

God. During this sweet process, two questions pop up the most.

The first is, "How do I *hear* God?"

Does God speak audibly? Yes, He is quite capable of it. Nevertheless, as we walk with Him through life, He speaks, for the most part, right *into* our minds. It's quicker and clearer.

Do not forget, we are not the only ones, obviously, He has to tend to. Untold numbers of us have pain we hope God will take away.

Yes, being patient is a virtue. But delaying communication with God reaps frustration and delays our healing. Being a squeaky wheel will help you receive the oil more quickly.

While having a heart-to-heart with God some time ago on this subject, I asked Him why He doesn't just speak audibly already!

His reply was, "I've not ever, nor will I, compete with the volume of the world."

It makes a lot of sense. When He does speak right to us, He wants us to understand immediately – and clearly – what He is saying.

Therefore, He speaks into our minds – with which, of course, we do all the good stuff like imagining, dreaming and creative thinking.

This is where many get a little confused, because God's voice mightn't rattle the rafters or shake the foundation as imaginations might anticipate.

We expect sacred communication from God to bowl us right over!

In 1Kings chapter 19, verse 11 the intrepid and resourceful prophet Elijah learned how to discern God's voice. He expected God to be in the blustering windstorm, the thundering earthquake and a massive, raging fire.

God was in none of them,

"... and after the fire a still small voice. So it was, when Elijah heard it, that he wrapped his face in his mantle and went out and stood in the entrance of the cave. Suddenly a voice came to him, and said 'What are you doing here, Elijah?'" (1Kings 9:12, 13)

God is that still, small voice that spoke directly to Elijah in a way he could and would understand. He spoke in a delicate whisper and asked the same type of questions you would expect a dearest friend to ask.

God will speak to us this way too, if we do the same to Him. It gives us the sensation of what I call a "gentle knowing." Suddenly we have words in our mind that are not a product of our own imaginative process. We are articulate with the Spirit.

Many times God will surreptitiously place a complete thought in our minds without any details or articulated words.

If we are open to receiving what He offers, we just miraculously *know* something is true, significant and profound – something we did not know before, but needed to.

Additionally, God will always speak the way we do. Do not expect him to speak Latin or 13th century

King James English. He simply speaks in the language, dialect or vernacular of the person with whom He is communicating.

If we speak English, so does He. If we speak Arabic, Welsh, Cajun, Danish, Miwoks, Ebonics, German, Chinese, Ilonggo, Spanish, Dingling, or any of the world's thousands of languages and dialects – so does He.

His main desire is for us to understand Him completely. He wants nothing of such import to get lost in translation.

The second most pressing question asked is, "How do I know if it is God I'm hearing speaking? Could it not be the devil, or even my own voice speaking inside my head?"

My response to this is two questions of my own, "Who are you addressing – God, or the devil?" and, "If you *were* talking to God, is the devil as prevalent and strong enough in your mind to come between you and God?"

People who answer yes to that question are actually admitting they have more faith in the devil's capacity to lead them astray than they have in God's ability to lead them in the way of righteousness,

"And when he brings out his own sheep, he goes before them; and the sheep follow him, for they know his voice. Yet they will by no means follow a stranger, but will flee from him, for they do not know the voice of strangers." (John 10:4, 5), and

"My sheep hear My voice, and I know them and they follow Me." (John 10:27)

With these scriptures in mind, it is crucial – and heartening – to understand that when God speaks, He strengthens and sooths us.

Even in correcting us, He comforts us.

When demonic forces, the systems of our corrupted, catastrophic world and even our own lost, impressionable minds – all enemies of our souls – speak to us, we are condemned, belittled, humiliated and found guilty.

Jesus, conversely, nurtures us, glorifies our achievements, understands our weakness and forgives our sins. He said we would run from the voice of the enemy, but we would know well His voice.

We should do both.

To test what we are hearing, we can repeat it aloud. If it's God, we know immediately. If it is not, we will know – as we speak it.

It is also a tremendous help to accept God's words while in a tranquil and receptive mindset. Many people are unable to still their minds enough to allow Him to get inside.

If that is the case, they must find ways to relax – and *will* their minds to be still.

Next, we verbally ask God our question. Now we listen, not with the fleshy ears on our heads, but from within. The next words or images that pass through our minds are from God, and therefore *are* God.

They must be spoken aloud so what we have received can enlighten, change, move us.

Remember that specific answers come from explicit questions. Generic questions will reveal little and yield nothing but frustration.

If we want a specific answer from God, we must ask a specific question and have the faith to believe that when we address God, He will hear, and answer,

"Call upon Me and I will answer you and show you great and mighty truths you do not yet know."
(Jeremiah 33:3)

The word "mighty" here refers to those powerful, irrefutable truths that are unreachable or inaccessible by any means other than from God himself,

"You cannot please God without faith, for you must first believe that He is and that He is a rewarder of those that diligently seek Him." (Hebrews 11:6)

Do not put God in a human box when talking with Him. His answers to our spoken questions can come in a variety of ways.

Allow God the freedom to answer any way He desires. But know this; He will answer.

After all, He is our God in Heaven and we are His self-imaged creations. He needs us to follow the leads of Jesus, but we are the ones who truly need Him, as a matter of survival.

We may receive actual words, or just a specific "knowing." He may show us mental pictures. If He does, they will possess great meaning, have immense feeling attached to them.

Now, speak what the mind picture means, what it feels like, and then listen to His reply.

When we confront Him with how we feel, and ask Him why we are in pain and where it originated, He will likely show us a harrowing, pain-inducing past remembrance.

Why? Because that's just what men and women essentially are – amazing, divinely wrought amalgams of their accumulated thoughts and past experiences.

Our pasts then are our lives' roots. Our past is our only reference point. The future is not here yet. The present becomes past, fast.

When God projects a picture of the past, do not resist or disregard it. Just look at it. Do not think about, analyze or judge. Just look.

The feelings we felt at the moment of the connected memory will surface.

When focusing on what that memory feels like, tell God what feels true in that memory. This is almost always different from what we now know to be true.

That's why it hurts!

That is the lie we believed at the inception of the memory. God will quickly respond to us when we tell Him what it feels like.

When God does answer, always repeat aloud what He is saying. When we speak what He tells us, it automatically records the truth over the established, excruciating lie.

Once that happens, the emotions stored in our memories change dramatically, and God frees us from pain by destroying the big lie.

Burning this process, based on Scripture, into our hearts is the only way to improve our mental health and spiritual equilibrium.

It is an excellent way to live up to the standards Jesus set and the only avenue to receiving what He promised to all believers – peace, quiet and confidence in this life.

Chapter Seven
Transformation, An Altar Experience

The only true physical work we can do for God is to offer up our bodies to Him as "living sacrifices." As we truly are born again, we are obliged to do so,

"I beseech you therefore brethren to present your bodies a living sacrifice... which is your reasonable service..."
(Romans 12:1)

Some translations structure the last part of this verse as "...which is your spiritual responsibility..." A subtle difference.

The word "sacrifice" here speaks of the ever-present potential of pain and suffering followed by an "altar-*altering*" experience.

This is not the altar at the front of the church but rather, the altar within the temple of God – the Christian,

"Or do you not know that your body is the temple of the Holy Spirit who is in you, whom you have from God, and you are not your own?" (1Corinthians 6:19)

Apostle Peter, in his own way of teaching, spoke of this experience in his first letter when he said, in no uncertain terms,

"Therefore since Christ suffered for us in the flesh, arm yourselves also with the same mind, for he who has suffered in the flesh has ceased from sin." (1Peter 4:1)

If we do not mentally prepare ourselves by gaining an understanding of what suffering is, its purpose, and how to work through it, we very well may run from the only One with the actual power to help us.

Unfortunately, this is what the majority of believers do. They miss Scripture's teachings of how to understand suffering.

The Church is good at reminding us of our problems, and the promises of God, but we so often miss hearing about the process of connecting to the power for the purpose of obtaining the promises.

I know very few Christians who don't want to live up to their full potential and reap the benefit spelled out in the first part of Philippians 3, verse 10,

"...that I may know Him (Jesus) and the power of His resurrection... "

However, we will only get to truly know Him better by living out the rest of the verse,

"...and the fellowship of His sufferings, being conformed to His death."

When Jesus walked the earth in His robe of human physiology, He suffered in the same way we suffer here now – in His soul.

He willingly, stoically and heroically faced absurd accusations, public denigration, serious persecution, condemnation and execution.

He did not defend Himself, blame others nor exact any sort of revenge. He did not fail His Father by taking any other, easier, route. Even accomplishing God's will was a point of suffering for Jesus, as it is for all of us who believe.

Through all His personal pain, anguish and crushing struggles, He constantly shared His grief with His Father, and obeyed everything commanded of Him.

So doing, He lived a sinless life, performed his works perfectly, qualified as our Savior,

"...but was in all points tempted as we are, yet without sin." (Hebrews 4:15b), and

"...who in the days of His flesh, when He had offered up prayers and supplications, with vehement cries and tears to Him who was able to save Him from death,

and was heard because of His godly fear, though He was a Son, yet He learned obedience by the things which He suffered. And having been perfected, He became the author of eternal salvation to all who obey Him." (Hebrews 5:7-9)

In 1Peter 4, verse 1, He requests we arm ourselves with the same mind, or – and here is that word again – attitude.

The world we live in is forever conspiring to make us believe we are not good enough as we are. As well, we all experience the agony of rejection, bum raps, personal injury and disrespect – the same horrendous sufferings Jesus endured.

The Holy Spirit's teaching through Peter and Paul is for us to offer ourselves to God as a living sacrifice when life becomes painful.

Why?

Because it is the only holy action we are able to take. When we instantly turn to God as we deal with the more awful wounds and battles of everyday life, we become more like Jesus by seeking Him.

He is the *only* One who can really help us.

By refusing to blame others for our inner pain and choosing to address the Lord with it instead, we indeed suffer in the flesh for a short time.

Then, according to 1Peter 4, verse 1 we have, in that moment, desisted from sin,

"...he who has suffered in the flesh has ceased from sin."

If we refuse to embrace our inner pain by trusting God through these moments, we will never see the glory of God,

"For I consider that the sufferings of this present time are not worth to be compared with the glory which shall be revealed in us." (Romans 8:18)

Nor will we transform in any way, or be able to discern God's perfect will for our lives,

"Do not be conformed to this world (this age), [fashioned after and adapted to its external, superficial customs], but be transformed (changed) by the [entire] renewal of your mind [by its new ideals and its new attitude], so that you may prove [for yourselves] what is the good and acceptable, and perfect will of God, even the thing which is good and acceptable and perfect [in His sight for you]."
(Romans 12:2 Amplified Version)

If we do not submit our pain to God, we persist in our self-directed attempts to defend and perfect our earthly existence, when we should be more worried about what's going on inwardly with our heavenly hook-up with Him.

This is the only road to spiritual maturity. It's James' rap in James 1 verses 2 through 4,

"My brethren, count it all joy when you fall into various trials, knowing that the testing of your faith produces patience. But let patience have its perfect work, that you may be perfect and complete, lacking nothing."

This is the only way to live a sinless life, for only in Christ is there no sin,

"Whoever abides in Him does not sin. Whoever sins has neither seen Him nor known Him. Little children, let no one deceive you. He who practices righteousness is righteous, just as He is righteous."
(1John 3:6-7)

As we continue speaking to Him – and obeying what He tells us to do – through the struggles of life, we abide in Him,

"Now he who keeps His commandments (immediate commands or directives) *abides in Him, and He in him. And by this we know that He abides in us, by the Spirit whom He has given us."*
(1John 3:24, author's comment)

Your Pain Is Showing!

In light of this, it is easier to understand why there is so much immaturity among members of the body of Christ. It also explains why there are so few who actually understand God's perfect will for their lives.

However, we need no longer fall prey to such lack of understanding. Hopefully we now understand how running from pain in life simply creates more pain.

Embracing our darkest moments of pain and presenting them to God invites Him to speak to the lies we believe, eliminating the pain.

It works to strengthen our relationship with God, which also increases our confidence in Him as He triumphantly delivers us into His ideal harmony.

This is what Jesus meant when he spoke so forcefully of sanctification by truth,

"Sanctify them by Your truth. Your word is truth."
(John 17:17)

Focusing on and living by absolute truth separates us from the world and keeps us free from sin.

We can live on that alone.

Chapter Eight
Pulling Down Strongholds

*E*xcuses, excuses!

Oh, how accomplished – and thorough – we are at concocting them. So thorough that "strongholds" is the military metaphor the Bible employs for the excuses we make for ourselves – because they can be monumental and unassailable.

They are, as well, *strong*. Our sadness, our sour moods, violent outbursts, fits of anger, or inability to put down that next Ron Bacardi and Diet Coke are wrought out of a sense of selfishness, boredom and hopelessness.

Scripture teaches us how to chisel away at these emotionally negative fortresses to build and fortify positive attitudes,

"For though we walk in the flesh, we do not war according to the flesh. For the weapons of our warfare are not carnal but mighty in God for pulling down

strongholds, casting down arguments and every high thing that exalts itself against the knowledge of God, bringing every thought into captivity to the obedience of Christ." (2Corinthians 10:3-5)

Strongholds are another primary cause of our ongoing struggle to know God's Truth.

They, like all of the physically catastrophic and spiritually imprisoning issues of modern life – and our attitudes and paradigms – are bred, formed, stored and held up in us, and correctable only from within.

They justify, or support, our bad behavior, words, and attitudes that "strongly hold" us back from shifting into positive gear and opening our hearts and minds to Jesus.

Human beings have the innate emotional need to feel desired, useful and necessary in the lives of others, especially loved ones and people we admire.

When we don't feel any of these things, our "natural man" creates strongholds to deal with the psychological conflict of living with inescapable and often debilitating feelings of worthlessness and/or loneliness in a vast, wild and wicked world.

Strongholds are rationalizations that have all kinds of applications, forms and uses. They cause folks to make statements like:

- *"I am not as bad as I used to be."*
- *"There are others worse than me."*

- *"If you knew what my father did to me you'd understand why I do what I do!"*
- *"If you'd been through what I have, you'd be angry too."*
- *"That's just the way I am!"*

Justifying our behavior blinds us to our need for change, effectively disrupting, if not totally derailing, the transformation process.

Until we bust-up, bulldoze and bury our strongholds, they keep us captives in prisons of our own making – the prison of our minds. Our strongholds construct the walls, and our justifications secure the bars restraining us.

Jesus came to free us. It is the heart and soul of His ministry – as found in Isaiah,

"The Spirit of the Lord God is upon Me, because the Lord has anointed Me to preach good tidings to the poor; He has sent me to heal the brokenhearted, to proclaim liberty to the captives, and the opening of the prison to those who are bound." (Isaiah 61:1)

The New Covenant provides us with not only the opportunity, but also the real-life responsibility, of doing the same works Jesus did – and then some,

"Most assuredly, I say to you, he who believes in Me, the works that I do he will do also; and greater works

*than these he will do, because I go to My Father.
And whatever you ask in My name, that I will do,
that the Father may be glorified in the Son."*
(John 14:12-13)

However, until we shake off completely our self-destructive attitudes and blow up our strongholds we are as ineffectual to Him as we are to ourselves.

We are wet dynamite, and our words and actions expose our attitude, good or bad.

As long as we have hot buttons that others can push at will, we won't be able to hear clearly the voice of God during the most devastating of life's tests and trials. We're too hyped-up to comprehend.

For this reason, the Apostle Peter urged to "arm yourselves with the mindset of Christ" in 1Peter 4, verse 1 and in chapter 5, verse 7, simply, to give our pain and cares to God.

Apostle Paul teaches us to be antithetical to the secular world by embracing the pain we feel as we "present our bodies to God a living sacrifice" (Romans 12:1).

Consequently, the bonfires of the ensuing transformation can be ignited, sparked, stoked and sustained by His truth,

"And do not be conformed to this world, but be transformed by the renewing of your mind."
(Romans 12:2)

Intentionally allowing God to deal with our aching souls develops our ability to hear Him clearly and respond appropriately.

Then we can do the works Jesus did.

Pulling down strongholds is agreeing with God that our attitude is not acceptable.

Like the alcoholic who finally admits – to himself and others – that his life is no longer manageable, we must realize the tremendous damage our bad attitudes are doing, to both others and ourselves.

When we agree with God on this point, He quickly moves us to absorb the next hard left jab life throws our way.

Chapter Nine
Casting Down Arguments

*T*he serious business of casting down our arguments has nothing to do with our every day petty disagreements with our peers.

It is, rather, about ongoing, often overpowering, devastating disputes we have with ourselves in our own hearts and minds.

We struggle for self-control by fighting mental and emotional battles with others as we relive and regret our painful experiences.

These arguments justify our bad behavior.

Incredibly, we work like maniacs talking ourselves into believing things we do not even *want* to believe in the first place.

Moreover, when we try to think the best, and employ some positive thinking, the "yeah-buts..." begin: "Yeah, but that person hates me and deliberately tried to make me look stupid and feel foolish, so I *must* deserve it."

This is a tragic waste of time and energy that does nothing but keep us self-absorbed.

Self-absorbed people cannot ever help others. They are unwilling or unable to find freedom from the second most powerful enemy tormenting them – themselves.

Self-protection drives narcissistic people.

They love, as much as hate, themselves. Their lives are "all about me." When others refuse to go along with their wishes or ideas, their behavior becomes as offensive to others as the pain that drives them feels to them. They don't care that they're obnoxious.

Science says that 70 per cent of all our daily mental activity is instinctual, but redundant and negative. From out of this area of activity, arise all the lame excuses and irrational arguments against any knowledge of God.

They all need immediate dismantling.

Knocking down arguments is simple. We refuse the temptation to try to figure out life for ourselves. We cannot treat our pain on our own. No new hobby, self-help class, drug or religion will assist us with that.

Until we willingly surrender to God and say, "I quit Lord! Why do I hurt so much? Where on earth is this pain coming from?" we will never truly know Him, or ourselves.

However, when we offer our pain to God as a living sacrifice, victory comes quickly,

"You are not restricted by us, but you are restricted by your own affections." (2Corinthians 6:12)

Your Pain Is Showing!

We find here yet again that the only thing alienating us from people and holding us back on any level is our own feelings.

We must give God control of them, and simply not allow them to control us.

Chapter Ten
Capturing Thoughts

Victory is always ours with sweet Jesus.

However, many of us will eventually find ourselves late in the fourth quarter of a do-or-die game against the imposing opposing squad of our big troubles and bad attitudes, led by the devil.

In this contest, we listen to Coach. Then we do what He says. That's how we are victorious in the championship game of life, the only way.

It is then, right there, that we learn to "bring every thought into captivity, to the obedience of Christ."(2 Corinthians 10:5b). We leave it all on the floor.

The English word "obedience" comes from the Greek word "hupako." It means, "to obey, listen to something; hearken, give heed, follow, yield; as a servant, soldier or pupil." Or teammate.

Taking every thought captive in light of the Greek text would cause 2Corinthians 10, verse 5b to read,

"And bringing every thought into captivity by listening, hearkening, giving heed to, following and yielding to Christ as His good servant, soldier or pupil."

If we do not hear what the Lord has to say about negative thoughts and inner arguments, we have not brought them into captivity into the obedience of Christ. They are therefore holding us up.

Obeying Jesus Christ is proof to Him and ourselves that He is our God and we are His messengers, servants, warriors, students, and most importantly, His sons and daughters,

"For as many as are led by the Spirit of God, these are sons of God." (Romans 8:14), and

"Blessed are the peacemakers for they shall be called sons of God." (Matthew 5:9)

Listening and obeying Jesus replaces fear and inner turmoil with His peace,

"Come to Me, all you who labor and are heavy laden, and I will give you rest. Take My yoke upon you and learn from Me, for I am gentle and lowly in heart, and you will find rest for your souls. For My yoke is easy and My burden is light." (Matthew 11:28-30),

"Be anxious for nothing, but in everything by prayer and supplication, with thanksgiving, let your requests be made known to God; and the peace of God, which surpasses all understanding, will guard your hearts and minds through Christ Jesus."
(Philippians 4:6-7), and

"You will keep him in perfect peace, whose mind is stayed on You, because he trusts in You."
(Isaiah 26:3)

Victory is ours when we begin living out 1Peter 5, verse 7 by casting all our cares upon Him. He takes care of our cares.

This is God's invitation to us to finally and firmly forge an intimate relationship with Him and to enjoy an open-door policy regarding approaching Him for help in dealing with the struggles of our lives and the trials of our souls.

When we accept it, we just *know* – we are no longer victims. We're riding high and dry.

We then vanquish our inner turmoil, and worries, turn to peace as we communicate – loud, aloud and proud – with the Lord.

When we are able to live high, above life's terrors, trash, temptations and turmoil we are victors in the love of Jesus.

We have heavenly championship rings.

This certainly does not mean, though, that once we've become Christians we will never again face losses, or problems of any sort.

They are certainties in our short seasons on earth – the bombardment of opportunities and challenges never stops. We have to defend our title.

However, as we learn to unload each contest onto the Lord as they occur, we escape and *overcome* our opponents just as Jesus did – one person, place, situation, thought and feeling at a time.

Overcoming the world is being able to live in perfect truth and peace in the middle of life's battlefields and the bombardment of lies,

"For to this you were called: because Christ also suffered for us leaving us an example, that you should follow His steps: 'Who committed no sin, Nor was deceit found in His mouth;' who, when He was reviled, did not revile in return; when He suffered, He did not threaten but committed Himself to Him who judges righteously." (1Peter 2:21-23).

PART II
PARADIGMS

Chapter Eleven
Purpose And Paradigms

Rotten attitudes do not just wreak havoc on our behavior. They color and shade the lenses through which we view our lives.

These lenses are our paradigms – the very framework of our philosophical and spiritual view of the world around us.

Applying the lessons of past experience to current situations invites misinterpretation.

They, in turn, and without fail, negatively affect our paradigms. Our lenses get clouded.

If a loved one, dear friend or co-worker mortally wounds us, the dark circumstances surrounding the act, and their outcome, will conspire to mess up our paradigms. The pain we feel seems unbearable.

These majorly messed-up paradigms make it impossible to see life clearly and truthfully, like looking at the world through a pair of broken spectacles – a disjointed blur of light and activity – at a life that isn't perfectly clear.

In Matthew 7, Jesus likens this state to having a speck in the eye, which causes us to miss the obvious,

"And why do you look at the speck in your brother's eye, but do not consider the plank in your own eye? Or how can you say to your brother, 'Let me remove the speck from your eye'; and look, a plank is in your own eye. Hypocrite! First remove the plank from your own eye, and then you will see clearly to remove the speck from your brother's eye."
(Matthew 7:2-5)

If we are resentful, we look at life through the splintered, bloody lenses of bitterness.

People whose paradigm is bitterness and fear usually feel like everyone else is out to "get" them. This is simple paranoia.

Those who are paranoid find it impossible to trust anyone, especially those closest to them. They are often convinced someone is watching or following them when they are not.

They hide when nobody looks for them.

Scripture says,

"...the wicked flee when no one pursues..."
(Proverbs 28:1a)

Paradigms built on fear and paranoia allow for anxiety attacks and feelings of panic. They then cause irrational decisions, foolish acts or complete psychological shutdown (no thoughts, actions or decisions, positive or otherwise, at all).

If paradigms are birthed out of fear, they might end up bringing about the very thing of which we are so terrified of facing.

If we are so deathly afraid of rejection, we naturally dance around others and distance ourselves from them, manufacturing reasons to dismiss them before we are dismissed.

At this point, turning our thoughts inward and relying on ourselves to think through our lives' worst problems, rather than directing our thoughts to a higher level – God – for our answers, is a major cause of depression.

Depression, on one level, is anger turned inward. Viewing life through the paradigm of depression is a dark, desolate and desperate, self-consuming way to live. No joy at all there.

Depression paradigms come from living too long with pain. When we feel alone, powerless or unprotected, we vainly attempt to over-control in an attempt at self-preservation.

If we fail, we plummet headlong into an increasingly deeper, heavier depression.

Exploring these types of paradigms leads us to look at Luke 11 verses 34 to 36,

"The lamp of the body is the eye. Therefore, when your eye is good, your whole body also is full of light. But when your eye is bad, your body also is full of darkness. Therefore take heed that the light which is

in you is not darkness. If then your whole body is full of light, having no part dark, the whole body will be full of light, as when the bright shining of a lamp gives you light."

The "eye" is in reference to the conscience – the access point for all the light we allow within us. The English word "good" in the previous verses comes from the Greek word meaning "single."

When our eye is single, in this context, our focus narrows to one specific thing – we are not looking at many things, or trying to live in two different, opposing worlds.

The only true light is from God,

"In Him was life, and the life was the light of men. And the light shines in the darkness, and the darkness did not comprehend it..."

"That was the true Light which gives light to every man coming into the world." (John 1:4-5, 9)

If we wish to be flooded with this life, light, and peace, we must be single-minded in our focus on God, the source of all we desire.

We accomplish our relationship with Him by receiving wisdom from His spoken Word and the Scriptures. In them, light represents truth and truth is the light of life,

"The entrance of Your words gives light; It gives understanding to the simple."
(Psalm 119:130), and

"Sanctify them by Your truth. Your word is truth."
(John 17:17)

Therefore, a single, or good, eye is one that allows in the light of God's ultimate truth.

If false promises and glittery temptations of the secular world captivate us, or we seek humankind's complex philosophies, self-help books or any other form of earthly "wisdom" for answers, our eyes fill merely with the darkness, not sublime kaleidoscopic color and God's pure white light. Pure illumination.

If our paradigms say we deserve a choice in life – and we alone can determine what is good for us – the darkness will prevail, and we continue to flounder,

"If therefore the light that is in you is darkness, how great is that darkness." (Luke 11:36)

Not to put too blunt a point on it, we are more than stumbling in the dark. We are outright fooling ourselves. Proverbs 14, verse 12 and Proverbs 12, verse 15 speak to this,

"There is a way that seems right to a man, but its end is the way of death," and,

"The way of a fool is right in his own eyes, but he who heeds counsel is wise."

Living with these nasty, negative emotions and perilous paradigms causes us to allow a pot-full of anger to simmer most of the time.

As our interactions with others and the normal stresses of life stir up these feelings, anger dives in like a seagull on steroids to protect us from experiencing the pain and fear that arises out of discrediting our paradigms. This should be avoided at all costs.

Anger, too, is a state-of-the-art power tool for the construction of fortified and airtight strongholds. Remember, though, any place that is remotely airtight will soon kill us if we try to exist inside it.

God's original purpose for the pain was to prevent us from putting ourselves in places or situations that have caused great harm to us in the past, in our old lives. It's to help us not be twice-bitten.

However, as Christians, we are born again and embarking on an incredible journey, with Holy Spirit rocket-fuel powering the ship.

We are not just natural, earthly beings any more, more like supernatural powerhouses – and within every one of us lives God,

"...the Spirit of truth, whom the world cannot receive, because it neither sees Him nor knows Him; but you know Him, for He dwells with you and will be in you." (John 14:17)

As His people, we have Someone higher, with ammunition infinitely superior to the sad, meager devices we use to protect ourselves.

God Himself has promised to protect us!

Gaining this supernatural protection only occurs, though, as we individually make Jesus Lord over every conceivable area of our lives – especially the areas that hurt.

We call on Him in our time of need. In the process, we build a relationship with Him. Emotional suffering, to Christians, is nothing more than an indicator that we believe a lie – the only thing that keeps us from God.

After God speaks to it, His truth wipes out the lie, the emotional pain instantly ceases. So for us, emotional pain is a doorway to God;

"The Lord is near to those who have a broken heart, and saves such as have a contrite spirit."
(Psalm 34:18),

"The Lord upholds all who fall, and raises up all who are bowed down." (Psalm 145:14), and

"The Lord is near to all who call upon Him, to all who call upon Him in truth." (Psalm 145:18)

He leads us ultimately to a peaceful life in Him – once we learn how to,

"…humble yourselves under the mighty hand of God, that He may exalt you in due time, casting all your cares upon Him, for He cares for you."
(1Peter 5:6, 7)

To experience success as Christians, we must learn to work with God in constructing solid new paradigms. And it's no huge revelation that godly paradigms come from godly attitudes.

Godly attitudes occur through a lifestyle of peace and inner tranquility – the place of rest from life's toils and traumas, referred to in Hebrews,

"There remains therefore a rest for the people of God. For he who has entered His rest has himself also ceased from his works as God did from His."
(Hebrews 4:9-10)

The rent for residing in that place of rest is constant fellowship and communication, with our Heavenly Father, as long as we dwell here in the world He created (see Psalm 91).

As we verbally communicate with Him, we can be shocked at how quickly it all happens.

We have attitudes and paradigm about all areas of life. Therefore, keep in mind – going through the next chapters – Peter's reminder in 1Peter 2, verse 21,

"To this, you are all called."

Your Pain Is Showing!

God is the only force powerful enough to adequately undo our airtight bad attitudes and design a new pair of paradigm-ical glasses.

Chapter Twelve
Swallowing Pride

*I*t is quite natural and healthy to be proud of our shiniest earthly accomplishments – especially ones that include helping or inspiring others less fortunate than ourselves. We can boast those a little.

As well, it is acceptable to be proud of our children – how they progress, how they obey us and how well they treat and respect others.

We should be proud of how our employers trust us. It is okay to be proud of our spouses, our church, our parents, our job or our talents – constructive pride makes it possible for us to be affirmative toward others. We can be proud of all the good we do.

Without it, we would rarely, if ever, tell others they are doing a good job or, conversely, have need of change. Confidence, part of pride, is good.

Pride is dangerous when we overestimate ourselves, thinking no one can do something better than, or as well as, we can.

When we reach the point of trying to manage life by ourselves, we are about to be destroyed by pride,

"Pride goes before destruction and a haughty spirit before a fall." (Proverbs 16:18)

So look out!

People will say, "I've worked hard all my life controlling my anger and coping with my issues so I could live a normal life. I'm proud I did it myself."

This is pride in self, and is destructive because it leaves no room for God,

"In the mouth of a fool is a rod of pride…" (Proverbs 14:3a), and

"A man's pride will bring him low…" (Proverbs 29:23a)

Feeling such a desperate need to do it ourselves is irrational, and comes from lies we naturally believe about ourselves and the lies taught to us by the world's myriad systems.

This is neither an acceptable lifestyle nor a mindset conducive to peace.

It is a concept that depends on humanity's insanely limited understanding of heaven and earth and even poorer judgment about our own lives,

"God gives grace to the humble while He resists the proud." (1Peter 5:5b)

If we don't humble ourselves we will never ask God to help us. If we don't ask God for help, we will never gain enough yards to score a spiritual TD and live in victory.

In denying our need for assistance, we are denying Jesus' Lordship over that area of our lives. By refusing to take our pain-filled issues to Him, we reject an intimate relationship with God and follow instead corrupt, shallow and meaningless religion.

This, in turn, causes us unnecessary pain as we choose to be "master" of our own lives.

Rather, we should ask God over and over again to reveal to us the truth.

Another failure rooted in pride occurs when we justify bad feelings with what others have said about or done to us.

It's always somebody else's fault, eh?

Another's misbehavior or malfeasance should never be justification for our bad feelings.

If that were so, Jesus would have been justified becoming furious – and no doubt fierce! – and making burro feed out of anybody crazy enough to accuse, publicly humiliate or bloody Him up in such a horribly malicious fashion.

That, of course, would have disqualified Him as our Savior. He wouldn't use His awesome power that way. Where would that have put the human race?

In a pickle, up the creek without a paddle, buns up, dead meat, outta luck, off playing a huge mug's game – that's where.

If another's actions make us furious or upset, we hand control over to them on a silver communion plate. Jesus overcame the evils of the world by understanding how not to fall prey to that temptation.

So can we.

When some people feel disrespected when others misbehave, they regard their actions as justification for frustration and a license to act out themselves.

This is a joke.

It's not overcoming anything. It is allowing other's failures to overcome us! Humankind's pride is why. However, God resists the proud and gives grace to the humble, says 1 Peter 5 verse 5b, followed by,

"Therefore humble yourselves under the mighty hand of God, that He may exalt you in due time."
(1Peter 5:6)

It is Jesus' passionate desire to lift us up, or exalt us out of our hurting position – not to chastise or belittle us for hitting rock bottom as most of us have, some more than others.

He will lift us in "due time." Some people think that this phrase means He will lift us up when He is good-and-ready, or when we have suffered enough for our mistakes, or after we have "paid" for our sins – or get punished.

None of these assumptions are correct.

In due time is the length of time necessary for us to humble ourselves, throw off our earthly inhibitions and call on Him – this second or years from now.

The choice is ours.

Due time arrives when we fully grasp the concept – however long that may take.

Feeling bad does not prove weakness, nor is it weak, humiliating, degrading or dangerous to express it. You "macho" men, you hunters: this statement was made especially for you.

We are a society filled with scared little boys hiding out in gym-chiseled adult bodies behaving like scared skinny, insecure little boys.

Women can freely and unselfconsciously express inner pain, sending a false message to some men that only girls should, and that real men don't cry.

This much misinformation causes men to hide our feelings, to the point of pretending we don't feel anything. This is living in denial – or, in the Bible, "deceiving" ourselves.

That said, I have helped men and women of all nationalities, occupations and lifestyles be released from years of emotional pain they could never even admit they had before.

After they fought through the idea they were actually in pain and became healed, they always admitted they thought their pain was just the way they were supposed to feel.

The real tragedy is that days or weeks or months later I'd see them again for another issue they hadn't taken to God because they thought they knew "where this one is coming from. This isn't like the last one."

This is both ignorance and pride in action. Is it not frightening how quickly we forget? No, it is worse than that – it is devastating to our lives and all those we touch. Cast all stupidity and arrogance therefore upon Him. Go right ahead!

It bears repeating – pride is the most impregnable obstacle to dealing with painful personal issues, because it prohibits us from asking God for help.

As long as we think we can do anything ourselves, that pride holds us back in every way. Pride of this sort keeps us in bondage because it makes it impossible for Him to intervene on our behalf and snap our chains.

God has given every one of us a free will. He cannot, nor will He, ever violate it. He wants, and needs, an invitation before He puts in a divine appearance at our pain-pulverizing parties.

It is no surprise, then, that understanding *how* to speak to – and then hear back from – God, is fundamental to forging a solid, living and breathing relationship with Him.

Knowing *what* to talk about is also helpful, and a good rule of thumb, when in doubt, is to go by what life feels like in the very moment of speaking to Him.

Rather than hide out and refuse to admit feeling anything, we must use emotions as a gateway to God.

Hey, people! Just tell Him how you feel and ask Him to reveal its source already!

You won't be sorry.

When we manage our bad feelings by reason, suppression or compulsive behavior, rather than unloading them onto the Lord's expansive shoulders, they co-opt thoughts, words and actions and poison our paradigms.

Therefore, our coping mechanisms, culled from our personal histories, popular culture and old wives' tales, make us live by pride, flee the truth and believe the lies about ourselves.

They allow our emotions and physiological impulses too much control over our actions and we end up living by earthly feelings and indulging lustful and basic natural urges.

This is being carnal-minded.

By taking those thoughts and feelings captive, we are being Spirit-minded. We allow God to replace the source of our compulsion with the truth.

Consequently, His work is *in* us, which brings about all the spiritual riches believers will experience throughout peaceful, prosperous lives on earth,

"Now the mind of the flesh [which is sense and reason without the Holy Spirit] is death [death that comprises all the miseries arising from sin, both here and hereafter]. But the mind of the [Holy] Spirit is life and [soul] peace [both now and forever].
(Romans 8: 6 Amplified)

It is important to keep in mind that we cannot cast all our issues on the Lord in one mega-ton emotional outburst (to "cast upon" means to fill Him in on all the things He needs to know – or *give* to Him, in communication).

Each problem has an origin and a life of its own and God repairs them individually.

We must then discuss with the Lord each issue that life brings our way as it occurs.

In appendix one, called Pinpointing Pain, I list eight simple steps to assist in the process of casting all cares upon Him.

I use these steps daily to deal with my own issues, and they are proving to be invaluable in making hurting people victorious in their battle against upheaval and inner agony.

The blessed process described here, lived numerous times daily by countless millions of people, works *every* time.

Incorporated into your daily lifestyle, it will amaze you as the Lord transforms every day into one of perfect peace and confidence in Him.

Imagine all the people living life in peace.

Chapter Thirteen
Bearing Critics, Taking Advice

*S*ome big-time attitude checks become real-live necessities when believers are criticized. Unfortunately, far to many don't take kindly to advice.

If Christians have trouble receiving either harsh critiques or even supportive suggestions from others, we quickly need to ask God why.

As always, we need Him to show us where this attitude began in our life, and then talk to Him to get rid of it – because it must go.

Whether the critic or advisor is right or wrong, older or younger, male or female – or simply on a personal power trip – is irrelevant.

The bottom line of *every* situation is our response to it, and how we arrive at it.

The religious leaders of Jesus' time were on the mother of all power trips. Without doubt, even worse (yes!) than today's top level leaders, for whom greed, politics or bigotry are primary motivations.

They were aware how much wiser the young carpenter was than they were, and how much more knowledgeable He was than them.

None had a clue, and they were aware they knew nowhere near as much about *anything* as He.

At only 12 years of age, His mother found Him in the temple sitting in the midst of the teachers and rabbis, listening, asking informed and intelligent questions (Luke 2:41-46).

The most amazing part of this account is that the Jewish culture of the time considered boys under the age of 13 to be children, and therefore not allowed the privilege of sitting with the religious leaders.

It was also exceptionally rare for them to allow a child to ask any questions at all. They must certainly have found the boy Jesus intriguing and challenging. Some translations assert that He was *debating* them.

All of this is meant to remind us of Jesus' response as He stood, beaten and tortured, unjustly accused and facing crucifixion,

"...when He was reviled, did not revile in return; when He suffered, He did not threaten, but committed Himself to Him who judges righteously." (1Peter 2:23)

To this, all of us are called.

Taking criticism and correction or advice indicates a heart that is pliable and teachable. The ability to do it is also a sign of, and a means to, growth and maturity,

"He who keeps instruction is in the way of life, but he who refuses correction goes astray." (Proverbs 10:17)

"Apply your heart to instruction, and your ears to words of knowledge." (Proverbs 23:12), and

"My son, do not despise the chastening of the Lord, nor detest His correction; For whom the Lord loves He corrects, just as a father the son in whom he delights." (Proverbs 3:11-12)

Unfortunately, justified criticism and punishment is commonly mistaken for personality altering, behavioral correction or mind re-training.

Admittedly, much of the time, because of our pain-driven and neurosis-nurturing world, it is hard to determine the difference.

In those situations, consider the following,

"He who guards his mouth preserves his life, but he who opens wide his lips shall have destruction." (Proverbs 13:3),

"So then my beloved brethren, let every man be swift to hear, slow to speak, slow to wrath; for the wrath of man does not produce the righteousness of God." (James 1:19-20), and

> *"If anyone among you thinks he is religious, and does not bridle his tongue but deceives his own heart, this one's religion is useless."* (James 1:26)

If another person's correction or criticism causes us to become angry or defensive, it is likely they have prodded the sleeping beast of a rancid lie within us. No mangy, sleeping dogs allowed.

However judgmental, rude or misguided we may perceive their "help" to be, we still need to ask the Lord from whence this feeling comes.

The righteous and proper attitude under such circumstances is humility, as is evident in the above verses, which say, "I will listen carefully and consider what you have said."

It is helpful to remember that correction, even when misguided, will primarily come from those who love and care enough about us to try to help us, tactfully or otherwise.

Try to maintain attitudes of thankfulness, even if the words are unbearably painful to hear, especially when the so-called critics themselves have a crappy, reprehensible attitude,

> *"In everything give thanks; for this is the will of God in Christ Jesus for you."* (1Thessalonians 5:18)

Remember that God *placed* the person prompting the hard issues we are facing, to help us. Unjust criticism from someone less knowledgeable or talented than we are, is just a tool God provides to work on our issues.

If we become angry or defensive, we risk destroying our witness by allowing our pain to incite us to negative actions and words.

Responding with negativity always causes us to miss a perfect opportunity to mature,

> *"My brethren, count it all joy when you fall into various trials, knowing that the testing of your faith produces patience. But let patience have its perfect work, that you may be perfect and complete, lacking nothing."* (James 1:2-4)

Every test- and trial-run God allows is a solid stepping-stone to spiritual and emotional maturity. It is surely the only way to reform our attitudes and correct our paradigms,

> *"For the ways of man are before the eyes of the Lord, and He ponders all his paths."* (Proverbs 5:21)

Are we able to admit freely when we are wrong? Can we, like our Jesus, remain stoic and serene when accused of being wrong even when we know we are right? Tough question, but,

> *"He who covers his sins will not prosper, but whoever confesses and forsakes them will have mercy."* (Proverbs 28:13)

It is undeniable that how we respond to our fellow human beings is indicative of how we respond to God. To be able to say, "I was wrong" not only indicates good character, it is essential to change,

"The ear that hears the rebukes of life will abide among the wise. He who disdains instruction despises his own soul, but he who heeds rebuke gets understanding." (Proverbs 15:31-32)

Even if we are falsely accused or unfairly criticized, it is important, for our personal and spiritual growth, to learn from the experience – even if it is only to ask the question, "How can I prevent this situation from happening again?"

"The fear of the Lord is the instruction of wisdom and before honor is humility." (Proverbs 15:33)

It takes tremendous humility to submit to someone who is rebuking us. To that end, willingness to learn from every situation in life is crucial to spiritual and emotional maturity.

If our desire is to one day achieve honor among our peers we must,

"…humble ourselves under the mighty hand of God that He may exalt us in due time as we cast all your cares upon Him knowing He cares for us."
(1Peter 5:6-7).

The inability, or refusal, to accept criticism, whether given fairly or not, is telltale – there are still lies we must deal with before our attitude can soar, and our paradigms brighten.

This is more than a good opportunity to allow God to help locate those same old lies.

It is a God-ordained moment.

We know the question to ask when life feels bad is, "Lord, where is this bad feeling coming from?"

Remember what the Word of God says,

"He who keeps instruction is in the way of life, but he who refuses correction goes astray." (Proverbs 10:17)

Because of the Scriptures that says,

"The steps of a righteous man are ordered of the Lord," (Psalms 37:23), and

"My son, do not despise the chastening of the Lord, Nor detest His correction; for whom the Lord loves He corrects, Just as a father the son in whom he delights." (Proverbs 3:11-12)

I will boldly make a guarantee: God *allows* every single person and situation to come across our paths, good or bad, for our benefit.

Everything that is, exists or happens is "Father-filtered." Take advantage of it.

Chapter Fourteen
Paying Due Respect

*U*nfortunately, far too many people have or had problematic parents who, due to the personal wounds they received in their own lives, made a reprehensible job of rearing them.

Regardless of their significant failure – and our feelings about it – the Bible is specific about how we are to deal with our parents,

"Honor your father and mother, which is the first commandment with promise: that it might be well with you and you may live long on the earth."
(Ephesians 6:2-3)

It is therefore important for us to consider, as Christians, whether we are treating not only our parents, but also everyone else in our lives, with the proper respect.

Is it possible to respect someone who may have disrespected us? If this is the question, it is only with God's help – and our unfailing desire to be in His perfect will – that we can ever expect to obey Him adequately in this regard.

There are far too many tragic examples of people, especially young ones, suffering or dying needlessly because they justify dishonoring parents – because of what they "did" to them.

I have seen young people disrespect their parents – ignoring their admonishments for simple personal safety – and die very young or at least prematurely as a result of deliberate disregard for them.

If a father or mother triggers bad feelings, though, don't ignore it, no matter how inappropriate or hurtful their behavior has been.

Seek God for His help.

Honoring parents does not mean acting as a whipping post or someone they can walk all over. Neither does it mean they are a best friend – or even a friend at all.

Honoring parents definitely does not automatically mean subservience to them.

Rather, honoring parents means refusing to speak ill of them, and ascribing value to them. They may have made an awful job of raising us, and damaged us emotionally in the process, but they still have value.

After all, God used them to bring *you* into this life. For that they deserve gratitude.

This may not seem like a blessing for those hurting at their own folks' bidding. However, once healed and aware of the possibilities life holds, they will be thankful they now exist – *and* are able to know and serve God.

* * *

If we are in an abusive situation, it does not honor God to quietly stay in it and not seek help. Moreover, those abusing others – that we know about – need our intervention.

As Christians, the best way to help them is to tell someone else what is going on. Once caught, the abuser often stops for good or at least opens up to God's assistance, be it court-ordered or not.

Abuse, though, like all human pain, never gets better by itself. Abusers rarely, without force or malice, seek help on their own.

If they are loved ones, help them out by letting someone know what is happening.

Typically, a spouse triggers painful inner issues, resulting in furious confrontations, out-of-control blow-ups or passive aggression and excruciating bouts of contagious chronic depression.

Those closest to us have the greatest ability to pull our triggers, so we either explode or withdraw back into our holsters to punish them.

Perhaps we rarely hold our frustrations in at home, and utter things to our families we would not dream of saying to our co-workers – or even total strangers on the street or those we don't respect.

If so, consider, for example, what God tells husbands about respecting their wives,

> *"Husbands, likewise, dwell with them with understanding, giving honor to the wife ...and as being heirs together of the grace of life, that your prayers may not be hindered."* (1Peter 3:7)

There are *no* exceptions or qualifications excusing husbands from totally honoring and respecting their wives, and vice versa.

Mutual difficult experiences should not be allowed to become excuses for obstructing prayers or our ability to be within God's perfect will for a marriage or a spouse.[10]

* * *

Our children, Psalm 127 tells us, are a heritage from the Lord – a reward and a blessing. A treasure. Yet they can also bring out in us the most fearsome emotional monster.

Look at what God calls fathers to do,

> *"And you fathers, do not provoke your children to wrath, but bring them up in the training and admonition of the Lord."* (Ephesians 6:4)

Do not be surprised, either, when children evoke in you negative feelings. It is no secret that they will

---

[10] Put the author's many years of experience to work in your marriage by acquiring his newest book, *Obtaining Marital Bliss,* soon to be available at www.LarryLow.com.

stop at nothing to impress peers or, many times, stage a personal rebellion against authority.

Above all, don't be shocked or stunned; no matter how dumb, disgusting or dangerous they are, into *not* discussing it with the Lord.

I deal with people who were physically unable to love and nurture their children because of the intolerable psychological feelings of horror they provoked in them.

One woman just felt "yucky and dirty" whenever she touched her eldest child.

Consequently, the saddest part of her life was how she had always treated her daughter. She could never tuck her in at night, hug her nor kiss her as she could her other kids.

She desperately wanted to love her eldest girl and she hated the anguish that not loving her had caused them both.

As her story unfolded, I discovered the woman got pregnant with her first child as the result of a vicious, long-remembered rape.

Later in life, as a single mom, she married, and with her husband produced several more children. The Lord revealed to her that her eldest child triggered a lie that said, "*I'm* dirty."

Once the Lord spoke His truth about the situation, destroying the glaring falsehood it generated, she suddenly found herself able to bestow upon her eldest child the love and affection she needed – just as she did the rest.

If kids trigger rage or negative feelings, do not overlook this or justify the feelings based on the child's childish behavior.

Ask the Lord to show you where your feelings got started in your life so you can fulfill the remainder of the verse we started with; Ephesians 6, verse 4,

"...but bring them up in the training and admonition of the Lord."

It is impossible to raise children in the admonition of the Lord if they trigger all sorts of ill feelings that incite you to evil actions

Bringing them up in the training of the Lord means to impress upon them that it is crucial to speak to God about personal issues.

Then we must teach them to communicate effectively with God; help them cast their cares upon the Lord. If we practice this so will they. If we do not, neither will they.

Another "family" relationship that begs consideration is with our Christian brothers and sisters. We can certainly get on each other nerves, and are rarely able to understand the psychological affect we have on each other.

Many times we fail to see that we are disrespecting, ignoring or aggravating them – or perhaps we do see, but do not, or will not, understand why.

Maybe we enjoy it a little.

When we find ourselves treating others with disdain due to their thoughtlessness, or some other weakness we detect in their character, it is a perfect opportunity to work with God to find the source of our own issue.

Once the Lord and we have taken care of our struggle they triggered within us, we can then turn to adequately help our brothers or sisters in the way Scripture instructs us,

"Since you have purified your souls in obeying the truth through the Spirit in sincere love of the brethren, love one another fervently with a pure heart," (1Peter 1:22), and

"Brethren, if a man is over taken in any trespass, you who are spiritual restore such a one in a spirit of gentleness, considering yourself lest you also be tempted. Bear one another's burdens, and so fulfill the law of Christ; for if anyone thinks himself to be something, when he is nothing, he deceives himself... Do not be deceived, God is not mocked; for whatever a man sows, that he will also reap." (Galatians 6:1-3, 7)

The word "trespass," or "fault," comes from the Greek word meaning "missing of the mark" rather than a transgression of law.

We have all missed the mark in life at one time or another. It's a fact that needs facing.

Rather than judge our brothers and sisters when they do the same, Scripture teaches us to "restore such a one" with gentleness, lest we also be tempted – as in our glass houses.

If we are unable to, and are compelled to hurl those psychic rocks because we take offense at, or are stressed out by, anyone else, it's a result of *our* issues, not theirs.

Chapter Fifteen
Accepting Authority

*S*ometimes Christians have to wonder just what compels us – like goofy, gentile Woody Allens – to so foolishly try to get away with thumbing our noses at authority of any kind.

It can make us, like lifelong New Yorker Woody attempting to drive on L.A. freeways, look pretty hilarious, or pathetic, sometimes – not to mention on the wrong side of the law.

Scripture is almost frighteningly clear that we are to respect those in authority,

"Let every soul be subject to the governing authorities. For there is no authority except from God, and the authorities that exist are appointed by God. Therefore, whoever resists the authority resists the ordinance of God, and those who resist will bring judgment on themselves. For rulers are not a terror to good works, but to evil. Do you want to be unafraid of the

authority? Do what is good, and you will have praise from the same. For he is God's minister to you for good. But if you do evil, be afraid; for he does not bear the sword in vain; for he is God's minister, an avenger to execute wrath on him who practices evil."
(Romans 13:1-4)

Many Christians might think they merely have a "delightfully irrepressible" rebellious spirit they are unable (and unwilling) to conquer.

Or, some think they might be possessed by demons, having even gone so far as doing "deliverance ministries" or "exorcisms," only to find out they change nothing. Most times, they make matters even worse!

Others believe their "sin nature" controls them, others convinced they are congenitally bad, even evil, and therefore unchangeable – "bad blood" they call it.

None of this is true for children of God.

As we become born-again, Jesus annihilates our sin nature, so evil no longer has even the slightest power over us,

"We know that our old (un-renewed) self was nailed to the cross with Him in order that [our] body [which was an instrument] of sin might be made ineffective and inactive for evil, that we might no longer be the slaves of sin." (Romans 6:6 Amplified Version), and

"In Him you were also circumcised with the circumcision made without hands, by putting off the body of the sins of the flesh, by the circumcision of Christ." (Colossians 2:11)

The devil and his infiltrators can no longer enter our imagination or make us do *anything*. We're above evil, temptation and reproach, as we live out of God,

"We know that whoever is born of God does not sin; but he who has been born of God keeps himself, and the wicked one does not touch him." (1John 5:18)

And the devil and his workers cut and run, like the yellowbellies they are, the moment we submit to God, affirming our firm stand,

"Therefore submit to God. Resist the devil and he will flee from you." (James 4:7)

Most times we give the devil excessive credit. We tend to forget that Jesus' finished mission on the cross whipped him so soundly,

"Having disarmed principalities and powers, He made a public spectacle of them, triumphing over them." (Colossians 2:15)

We profit from Jesus' work when we accept Him, no delay or doubt, as our Savior.

Our feelings, as we are now aware, drive everything we say, think or do – disrespecting authorities is no exception. That's common.

Law officers on every level, for many oppressed souls, stir up attitudes of disrespect. Most times, it is because of a wrong suffered in their past at the hands of the local constabulary.

This causes them to feel unsafe in their presence. The cops freak 'em out.

Others grew up with parents or caregivers who had little or no respect for the police, and they suffer from the same bad attitude toward all authority figures. They carry huge chips on their shoulders.

Only God knows, of course, where that angry feeling originated. Ask Him to reveal it and to speak to that (new or used) lie.

The person who is impossible to respect is simply triggering one of those treacherous lies.

Once again, take the time to ask God the most important question we ever ask, "Lord, where is this pain coming from?" It is never prudent to assume *we* know our pain's origin,

"And if anyone thinks that he knows anything, he knows nothing yet as he ought to know."
(1Corinthians 8:2)

Struggling at submitting to authority is tantamount to struggling to submit to God. Not submitting is an expression of lack of trust in Him.

By not trusting God, we will be more likely to run when the going gets tough – or quit when He tries to do something big in us. Winners, though, never quit.

If we do quit, we will lose. We will never realize the bountiful nature of what God can so easily do for us – or through us – which is necessary to experience the joy of the Lord.

When we fully submit to God, trusting Him with our lives, we become responsible Christians and that is when we quit blaming everyone else for how we feel. That's not the righteous attitude.

We must now stop giving others power over our lives and speak, audibly, to the Lord (follow steps in the appendix one).

No one will ever regret it!

Chapter Sixteen
Living Love

*T*here is one essential kind of love that our second-millennium world knows little about.

It is, simply, God's incredible love for his beloved children and most dazzling creations.

Known in the Bible as "agape"[11] love; this love is spoken of in Jesus' command,

> *"…love one another; as I have loved you, that you also love one another."* (John 13:34)

We should always hold this type of love in our hearts and minds – not just for God, but also for friend *and* (perceived) foe alike.

---

[11] For more detail about walking in agape love and purifying the soul, read *Genuine Christianity*, by L. F. Low, (American Book Publishing Company), 2009 available at www.LarryLow.com, www.genuinechristianity.org, or Amazon.com.

We know about and possess great love for our family and dear close friends. Few of us have escaped the perennial slings and arrows of romantic love.

We love our cultural heroes, especially the ones who do the right thing.

None of it is anywhere near perfect love. Biblical agape love, however, is.

Agape love is God's. Mankind cannot manufacture this kind of love, or experience it on our own.

It only comes from God.

Loving people who also inhabit this world, though, on any level, is a concept that causes great apprehension, fear and concern among many calling themselves Christians.

We tend to love one another intellectually. It is impossible to obey Jesus' admonition to love (agape) others while harboring hostile or discordant feelings. We labor to "be loving" rather than actually living out God's perfect, effortless love,

"Since by your obedience to the Truth through the (Holy) Spirit you have purified your hearts for the sincere affection of the brethren, (see that you) love one another fervently from a pure heart."
(1 Peter 1:22 Amplified)

It is a love that cannot be lived on our own power. According to Peter, we also cannot love others the way Jesus did until we "purify our souls" – referred to many different ways and umpteen places in Scripture.

Romans 12, verses 1 and 2 contains other pertinent references to purifying the soul, otherwise called "renewing your mind."

John 17, verse 17 refers to purifying our souls as "sanctification by truth" and in Philippians 4, verses 6 and 7 it is referred to as "receiving the peace that passes all understanding."

Loving others with God's agape love is giving to others what God deems *necessary* in any given relationship at any given moment.

If you do not hear God clearly, you cannot love others the way He instructs you.

In John 7, verse 38, Jesus says that "rivers of living water" (love and truth) would flow from the heart of those who believe.

We are God's conduits, or pipelines, to the dry and thirsty world. Even so, we clog our own hearts and souls with the impurities of the lies we believe, and we pollute the ever-fresh, living water of God as it flows through us.

When issues trigger our bad attitudes, we inject those toxins into the pure thoughts and words spoken to us by God, and in most cases, because of our pain, we miss totally what He is saying.

The parched and poisoned world around us needs the pure, untainted, living water – or agape love – from Heaven. It is the Christian's blessing and responsibility to pour it into the cups of all who will freely drink it in.

In other words, we are obligated to purify our souls so we can deliver what the world is waiting for –

God's life-giving, truth-bearing flow of sanctifying water, or His *love*.

Lies believed to be true create in us much mental clutter and psychic impurity.

When we finally replace them with God's truth we are shocked and delighted at the liberation we feel through purified souls.

Chapter Seventeen
Winning At Work

*D*o you need to check your locked, loaded and potentially deadly attitude toward work – what you do, how you do it, where you work and for what/whom – at the door?

It is amazing how often people complain about their employers, their amount of pay, when they get time off, their benefits or lack thereof and their distant parking space.

They don't realize that all manner of work is honorable, and God expects us to carry our own weight and provide for our families.

They tend to forget how sufficient their current compensation looked when they were unemployed and all they had was time off.

They forget that involuntary free time isn't what it's cracked up to be, which is why they went looking for a new job in the first place.

Some ought to remember how grateful they were when their employer first said, "You're hired! You start Monday."

Our attitude as Christian employees should be as grateful now as when we were hired.

After all, didn't we agree to what our pay would be, what the job requires, the hours we would work and when we would have time off?

The Scriptures teach us how to respond to our employers and the work we do for them,

"Bondservants, (employees) *be obedient to those who are your masters* (employers)*according to the flesh, with fear and trembling, in sincerity of heart, as to Christ; not with eye-service, as men-pleasers, but as bondservants of Christ, doing the will of God from the heart, with good will doing service, as to the Lord, and not to men, knowing that whatever good anyone does, he will receive the same from the Lord, whether he is a slave* (employed) *or free* (self-employed).*"*
(Ephesians 6:5-8; comment the author's)

Might it also work against us if we treat our employer poorly? What would the Lord say about our complaining about, running down, or belittling our employers?

Not, "Well done!" obviously.

If this is a concern, as with all other earthly issues, ask the Lord why and where the negative feelings about employment began.

We must work with Him to change our attitude before we damage or destroy our witness as a Christian, our future as employees or our chances of a brilliant, or at least gratifying, career.

Are we lacking confidence concerning our work or the ability to accomplish what our employers' desire from us? Do we fall short of our own expectations of ourselves? Do we even care?

Do we complain about how unfair our bosses are in that others seem to get all the breaks while none come our way?

Do we do as little actual work on our jobs as we are able to get away with?

On the other hand, are we workaholics?

These are all obvious symptoms of pervasive emotional pain that either drives us forward or holds us back. Of course, only God knows the origin of what we are feeling.

I suffered from feelings of inadequacy, which drove me to be a workaholic. I couldn't deal well with the tenuous situations at home so naturally I worked constantly, as an escape from it.

These two pressures "forced" me to work all the time – in my mind I had no choice but to jump at every picky little need my employer had or every suggestion my superiors made, whether it was my responsibility or not.

All of this inner upheaval and fear, and the extra stress it put on my home life, was caused by the one little lie that I had securely tucked away in my subconscious memory of working with my uncle and dad as a young boy.

Your Pain Is Showing!

Had I not talked to God about the feelings and received His truth, which made me free, the following chain reaction would have surely occurred in my life.

Life as it was would drive me crazy. My marriage would face demolition, and my children would never be able to face me again, as I would be spending all my earnings on bourbon.

My dear grandchildren would never have a healthy example of a functional home.

My wife would be miserable alone and I would still be in misery, driven by my inner demons, pains and fears – that is, if I had not already put the metallic-tasting muzzle of a .38 revolver in my mouth and pulled the trigger.

There is no doubt. One lie, believed by one person to be true, has the potential to ruin every life it touches.

Chapter Eighteen
Family Matters

We always treat those nearest and dearest to us the harshest. It's terrible, what we do.

Why is this? Concisely, it is a matter of proximity. They're always there, we're comfortable with them, and they provoke feelings of guilt and inadequacy more quickly than anyone else.

They are those who love us most, know us best – the ones we most want to impress.

Another reason has to do with our ability or inability to escape from pressure building at home. Our families are much harder to run from than colleagues or casual acquaintances.

The phoniest, most pathetic example of a modern Christian is he or she who preaches the lessons of Jesus to their family but lives something far less, and often more evil, out of their sight.

Our own private lifestyles and the daily, dedicated presentation of our own faith speak louder than our verbal message.

Your Pain Is Showing!

The church leaders, evangelists and those in the pews should be less concerned with the showbiz glitz – and monumental monetary motivation – of preaching convictions and more with living them.

If they want to preach, they should preach the Gospel. If they preach the Gospel, they must live it with the same, preferably genuine, passionate intensity they claim to possess.

One old, familiar theme among hurting believers is that the parents often hold higher standards of behavior for their kids, a lifestyle purer than they are willing to live themselves.

This hypocrisy – of caregivers and church leaders alike – might cause those who witness it to question seriously their own faith, or to turn right away from God altogether.

If you are going to talk the talk with your family, then for goodness sake, at *least* walk the walk in the manner you expect of them.

Do not be a hypocrite!

Struggling in our relationship with God or the church doesn't justify forcing our spouses or children to perform to make us look good.

Being a genuine Christian means we teach and lead families by example.

Alas, many husbands clutch to this messed up paradigm concerning the meaning of their wives' submission to their husbands.

This type of man generally, even if falsely, considers himself as the "boss" or lord of the family.

He might also be unwilling to accept any other interpretation of the marriage.

Only rarely does he consider his wife to be an equal partner, or hear her opinions on any matter, or worry about her feelings.

Scripture clearly reveals God's view of men's roles in dealing with their wives,

"Wives, submit to your own husbands, as to the Lord. For the husband is head of the wife, as also Christ is head of the church; and He is the Savior of the body. Therefore, just as the church is subject to Christ, so let the wives be to their own husbands in everything. Husbands love your wives, just as Christ also loved the church and gave Himself for her that He might sanctify and cleanse her with the washing of water by the word, that He might present her to Himself a glorious church, not having spot or wrinkle or any such thing, but that she should be holy and without blemish. So husbands ought to love their own wives as their own bodies; he who loves his wife loves himself. For no one ever hated his own flesh, but nourishes and cherishes it, just as the Lord does the church."
(Ephesians 5:22-29), and

"Let the husband render to his wife the affection due her..." (1Corinthians 7:3)

God has ordained man as the "head" of his wife – just as Jesus is ordained as Head of the church, or His body – but they are equal in God's eyes in that they are the same flesh as their husbands. To God, equal.

In no way does this eliminate the wives' responsibility to build a personal relationship with the Lord to enhance and help her find true intimacy with Him as with her husband.

Wives should submit to husbands *as* they submit to the Lord. Do you see it, gals?

Women are to submit to their husbands the *very* same way they submit to God, with love, faith, and compassion.

Men, headship means responsibility for our wife's emotional and spiritual security, as well as their earthly happiness on all levels.

Men are to deal with their wives in the same manner Jesus deals with the church.

He does not browbeat the church into submission; neither does He expect anything from the church that He would be unwilling to do. He cheerfully serves it.

Jesus is continuously revealing His nature, as well as the secrets of the Kingdom of God, thus cleansing us by His word of revelation,

"...that He might sanctify and cleanse her with the washing of the water by the word." (Ephesians 5:26)

He responds to the broken hearts of His followers, bringing them emotional security.

Husbands have the same responsibility to separate, sanctify and spiritually cleanse their wives through the purification of the Word they personally receive from the Lord.

If we are not receiving revelation from the Lord, we cannot fulfill that responsibility.

When a man is alert to the emotional needs of his wife and shares with her the revelations the Lord is showing him, she finds herself spiritually and emotionally secure.

This growing security and sanity builds confidence in her husband's place in the Lord, and she becomes much more able and willing to submit herself to him as to the Lord.

Such a three-way interaction between the Lord, wives and husbands should become a lifestyle – a continuous act of receiving from the Lord and sharing it with our spouses.

This lifestyle will continue, and may only end, when the Lord calls us to be with Him.

Young couples might wonder how they might quickly receive such revelations from God.

They can do it by looking to Him for personal edification and growth, communicating hard issues to Him, and seeking His guidance and strength,

"Therefore humble yourselves under the mighty hand of God, that He may exalt you in due time, casting all your care upon Him, for He cares for you."
(1Peter 5:6-7)

It is understandably difficult for a woman to submit to her husband as she does to God unless her husband enthusiastically follows the Lord and actively works to develop his own relationship with Him.

One horrible family paradigm, which far too many men subscribe to, says, "I bring home the bacon. My wife does all the praying."

This is exactly backwards according to Scripture. And we shake our head over the disintegration of family in modern society!

When things are out of order, we have chaos, unbridled sinning and evil influences, not the desired quietude and confidence.

If the father figure in a family considers household duties to be "women's work," then the children probably have the same messed-up, stinkin' thinkin' that breeds disrespect, if not contempt.

If dad beats his wife or kids, they will most likely absorb that behavior as well.

I have witnessed men valiantly champion the cause of Christianity and the importance of equality for their wives within it, while refusing to help their wives clean up around the house or take care of their kids.

They believe it to be beneath them, or too much of an insignificant act to clean house, certainly the toilets, or cook, wash dishes, make a bed.

Among the majority of the men who feel this way, I also noticed they were not opposed to having their wife work out of the home as well, to help bring in enough money to support the family in the style to which they had become accustomed.

This kind of bad paradigm not only causes problems between the husband and wife but also between sons and their future wives.

When wrong paradigms mess up families, it sets a damaging example to future families. It is a domino effect. The sins of our fathers.

Understanding the proper order of the proper family paradigm is only half of the corrective measure. It's just talk.

The other half is how much we are willing to *do* to arrive at it, and then actually go with what we know is the right thing. It's called walking the walk.

Real change never comes easily when we attempt it alone. However, when we cry out to God we have His assurance as Christians that He will help us,

"Come to Me, all you who labor and are heavy laden, and I will give you rest. Take My yoke upon you and learn from Me, for I am gentle and lowly in heart, and you will find rest for your souls. For My yoke is easy and My burden is light." (Matthew 11:28-30)

We're not alone, nor need we do it alone.

The time to exercise, and thereby declare, our faith in God, and ask for help, is now.

Let Him make the major changes *easy*.

* * *

So far, we have been hitting men hard in the area of family paradigms due to the importance they play on future generations and their responsibilities within the family God has given them – and deservedly so.

There is *no excuse* in God's eyes to harm your wife, or any woman, physically.

Domestic assault is one of modern times' most common everyday atrocities. Most times women don't even tell anyone it happened, for fear of more, severe injury.

This societal atrocity causes a destructive paradigm shift in the minds of women in general; they expect less from their men than God has instructed men to live up to. They've "settled" for what they have.

Abuse at a man's hands makes women in general distrust all men – in *general*.

Their justified mistrust, rooted deeply in what they believe about themselves, keeps them from submitting to their husbands on any level, no matter how hard the man tries to change or how closely he follows the Lord.

* * *

Pain is at the root of the perennial human propensity to negatively judge cherished loved ones (something we ought to leave to God).

It also makes us justify our pigeonholing of everyone else into unjust and hurtful ethnic or sexual stereotypes, when we don't look at the soul.

This makes it nearly impossible for us to deal with one another, or anyone in our lives, justly.

It's *our* way or the highway, see?

No! It most definitely is *not*! If we need to ascribe labels to everyone different from us in region or religion, we have seriously whacked paradigms that will, if left unattended, lead to outright bigotry on our part. This is most inexcusable.

Not a good family paradigm.

If bigotry starts to bear its bloody teeth in our attitudes, especially within our families, we have a *most* dire need for the Lord God to correct us. Fast.

Chapter Nineteen
Sex And The Christian

*T*hey say in advertising, "sex sells."

Well, as Christians, we're just not buying. Never should, nor would, we trade on this most significant and sacred part of our earthly lives.

Regardless, sex is everywhere.

It is, then, no huge surprise that many people stumble and become mortally frightened in that area – be it in attitudes toward sex itself, unsettled feelings toward the opposite sex or stress and confusion about sexual identity.

Improper attitude regarding this crucial article of our covenant with God is spiritual suicide. That said, we need God's immediate attention first to address and then alleviate our profound misapprehension about sex.

Since the "Swinging '60s," our society has come to consider casual sex as a major part of humankind's recreation, rather than a holy gift from God for the purpose of procreation.

This has cheapened, decimated, and then outright ruined society's paradigms about sex, sexuality and the value of life itself.

Because of the endless bombardment of evil temptations society promotes, our paradigms concerning sex may very well fall in line with our culture's – a careless disregard of the sanctity of the sexual act, the promotion of "free love," and selling consumer products with the physical allure of sex.

If this is the case in your life, you badly need God to speak some serious truth about sexuality and the proper, healthy role of sex for men, women and yourself. We can't avoid it.

If a man's paradigm regards women as playthings created for his pleasure, not only is he a boor and a blockhead, he needs to find out where this pattern of thought began and ask the Lord to speak truth to it, and eradicate that lie – but quick!

If he believes God created women for men as nothing but objects of casual companionship and entertainment, requiring – and deserving – nothing in return (unless of course they work as professional sex providers, another manner of sinful behavior altogether), he will likely not develop any kind of healthy relationship with any women.

It couldn't be purer or simpler.

Fathers and mothers will most certainly do an inadequate job of guiding young daughters through their arduous ascent to womanhood, or teaching sons how to be what we used to call "gentlemen."

There are so few of them left.

This recreational-ization of sex has also brought into prominence dangerous attitudes about the swift termination of "inconvenient" pregnancies, better known as abortion.

It is common knowledge, among Christians and medical professionals alike, that a fetus's brain is developed and functional a mere nine weeks after conception, and is capable of responding to stimuli by the 24th week.

By that time, the child has also developed fingerprints – proving that even this early in existence, he or she is, to be sure, an individual, unique among all other *living* beings.

God has already given the baby its identity. At that point, the baby's brain is already busily interpreting a huge flash of new experiences.

Whether born into poverty, to improper parents – or is unwanted, just tolerated, much wanted, loved or cherished – the baby *lives*.

Abortion, then, to the born-again believer, is murder – the ending of a human life. Murder robs a person of life, liberty and the personal pursuit of happiness, and is the 6th Commandment, the most mortal to break.

Beyond that, there isn't much more to say about it that is in any way relevant.

Because society's overall sexual paradigm is askew – warped by pornography, tainted by Hollywood, intensified by everyday contact with sexual images – we lose sight of the true definition of love; what it is, what it is not.

Contrary to contemporary belief, sex does not prove love between two people. If it did, the divorce rate in North America would not be at 60-some per cent. There would never be a single case of rape on the police logs.

I have ministered to young women who believed they could make a man love them by giving them anything – including body and soul – they wanted.

Women, in particular, should take notice. We simply can't *lead* anyone to truly love and cherish us, any more than we can make an impertinent palomino quench its thirst.

If we must first sell ourselves (or worse, give ourselves away) in hopes of being loved, we are not being loved at all. Love is giving to others, not taking from them.

If a man will casually accept the gift of sex out of wedlock from a woman (or demand she give it to him) before they say, "I do," he must not love her very much.

The only time sex is right is when we give ourselves because we *know* we are committed to our partner for life, not as a bargaining chip to acquire somebody's love.

For Christians, love is giving to another – wife, husband, partner, spouse, significant other, loved ones, etc. – precisely what God deems necessary for their betterment.

If, like the (likely male) lion's share of the world, we believe it takes an act of sex for someone to prove love for us, then we must ask God, once again, where that dangerous and unfounded belief started.

If we are trying to *make* someone love us, we should ask God why, and to show us what makes us feel unloved, or unlovable.

That same lion's share usually suffers from serious issues of inadequacy or abandonment. In which case, they will never have healthy relationships with anyone, let alone a partner with whom they plan to spend their lives.

These unwitting unfortunates will never have proper self-esteem until they understand the truth about themselves.

* * *

If we believe it is normal and acceptable to live the bi-sexual, homosexual or lesbian lifestyle, we are standing unwittingly in the firing line with an ever-growing portion of our ever-more-permissive society.

The prurient piper will be paid.

Unfortunately, the school of thought who thinks he will not has found acceptance within a faction of what the modern world calls the "church," which is as utterly *wrong* as a religious organization can be, says the Bible, the very Word of God.

How can this be?

Simple; they are simpletons. They have no understanding of homosexuality and therefore no clue how to assist anyone wanting freedom from his or her predilection.

Rather than stand firm on Scripture, this "church" chooses compromise instead, and fails, consequently, to learn to rescue people from destructive practices and lifestyles.[12]

This is ridiculous and dangerous, obvious by what God says about this extremely contentious matter,

"...for a man to lay with another man as with a woman and for a woman to lay with another woman as with a man, is an abomination."
(Leviticus 18:22; Leviticus 20:13), and

"Therefore God also gave them up to uncleanness, in the lusts of their hearts, to dishonor their bodies among themselves, who exchanged the truth of God for the lie, and worshiped and served the creature rather than the Creator." (Romans 1:24, 25)

Finally, Revelation 22, verses 14 and 15 are unequivocal and specific,

"The sexually immoral will be found outside the Holy City, cut off permanently from God after the creation of the new heaven and new earth."

---

[12]Restoration Ministry Training information and materials are available on www.LarryLow.com. Click on 'DVDs' then *'Restoration Training Materials.'*

Your Pain Is Showing!

Why God is so forcefully set against such a seemingly harmless lifestyle is no mystery.

The Bible explains it plainly by saying it is because of homosexuality's un*natural* nature.

It goes dead against His natural order of things.

So that's it. It's just that simple, despite surprising recent ELCA actions.

God's natural order is sex for procreation as found in the book of Genesis. Any practice that discourages this, or encourages needlessly spilling precious seed onto the "ground," is unnatural, unclean, and so, an abomination. The Lord does not like this.

God deems homosexuality unsafe and unclean for the obvious reason that it can spread disease and consequently kill the innocent.

It also, since conception cannot occur, slows the propagation of the human race, and if everyone indulged in this practice, it would eventually terminate God's creation.

It is extremely important to note, though, that He is *not* calling the people who practice these unnatural acts abominations. Only their deviant sexual acts are abominations.

God says hate just the sin, not the sinner.

Many accuse God of making mistakes by placing women in men's bodies and men in women's bodies, which implies homosexuals are a third type in His creation or their own special sexual species.

If this is true, and I don't believe it is, then God is an unjust tyrant who demands certain standards of behavior, but makes it impossible for many of his servants to comply.

If God made mistakes in creating us, then He's not perfect. If He's not perfect, He can't be God.

If God is not God then it just does not matter how we behave. All that we have learned and accepted from the Bible would be an out-and-out lie.

I do not believe this for one second. I find it difficult to believe any rational mind would.

Ultimately, if it was God at fault, we are released from responsibility and wrongdoing. Sin would not exist. We'd love it!

It is no secret that we have been trying to blame God for our own miserable failings since the beginning of time,

"Then man said, 'The woman whom You gave to be with me, she gave me of the tree, and I ate.'"
(Genesis 3:12)

All of the above is why we need a Savior. In the natural world, without Him we will never be at peace with God or with ourselves.

Because so many Christians are bereft of peace and well-being, we adopt many and any substitutes that give us a false heightened sense of importance or a few minutes of sensual pleasure.

This is such a misguided attempt to catch the fleeting thrill of grabbing the big brass ring, not God's eternal golden grace.

Your Pain Is Showing!

So-called deviant sex is just another of the litany of coping mechanisms society accepts in the hopes of finding perfect inner peace.

In our degenerating world, the "free love" sexual revolution of the '60s has caused, ultimately, more sorrow and problems than it solved.

If we are sexually adrift, questioning our sexual orientation, or have difficulty relating to the opposite sex in a healthy way, it is because of damaged subconscious emotions and off-balance spiritual life.

Sexuality is a potent detriment to peace if it is causing conflict in the soul.

Unrequited love alone has caused men and women to end their lives on earth rather than live without the one who has – yes! – *rejected* them.

But take heart. When one's emotional wounds heal, and life regains its equilibrium in Jesus, everything else in life falls into place.

PART III
PATIENCE

Chapter Twenty
The Old Mirror Test

Are you able to look at your face in the mirror and declare with any conviction, "God is doing a great job. I am happy with you. You are okay just the way you are!"?

If not, you have a self-esteem issue, which will hold you back and ruin your future.

Some folks actually hate themselves – or at the very least dislike – and remain dissatisfied with how they look, behave or treat others because of lies they believe about themselves.

God knows when and why they accepted these falsehoods, and will show them if asked.

Rarely does a person who dislikes him or herself care about the feelings of others, never mind their own. They're on a destructive path.

So often they try to punish themselves for this with self-inflicted bodily pain or injury.

Your Pain Is Showing!

They typically feel inadequate, worthless or stupid, which justifies their self-destruction – they want to hurt themselves to hurt others.

When I was a young man, I could not look at myself in the mirror without thinking,

"Man, you are such a huge dork – you're also ugly, dense, and useless to anyone."

I'd no idea why I felt that way. Many years later I was shocked to discover I believed a lie – that I was inadequate.

My feelings of inadequacy originated from the incident I describe in chapter two, when I misinterpreted an experience I had as a nine-year-old working alongside my dad and uncle.

As a young boy, of course, my parents did not expect me to keep up with the work the men were doing. But I, like most nine-year-olds, to impress my dad and uncle, still tried.

Naturally, I was unable to come close to doing what *I* thought I should be able to do.[13]

That normal, everyday experience almost ruined my life; not because of the harshness of the incident,

---

[13] I have observed many times that children want to do everything by themselves when they are too small to do anything. (Conversely, by the time they are old enough to do most things by themselves, they do not want to do anything without help!) This mindset causes children to misinterpret their abilities without any consideration of age, mental capacity or physical size. They believe lies about themselves that negatively affect their future. An observant parent or caregiver can help the children escape this dilemma by encouraging them to hear the truth from the Lord.

but because I misinterpreted the experience by believing I would never be good enough no matter how hard I tried.

To such a young boy, this was an absolute truth. I could not keep up with the men, but my interpretation did not alleviate my shame due to natural circumstances of age and size.

I simply believed from that time on that no matter how hard I tried my efforts wouldn't be good enough to succeed at anything.

This drove me to workaholism from a very young age. In my adult years, I also became a bitter, angry and ultimately suicidal alcoholic.

God's mercy freed me from alcohol when I chose to follow Him. No one, including me, knew what I believed about myself after that fateful day of trying to impress grown-ups with my sorting gate finesse.

I was a teenager before anyone realized I was not a very happy young fella. By that time, I had lived through other normal (to anyone else) experiences that confirmed the subconscious belief that I would never be "good enough."

As I maneuvered myself into adulthood, the most insignificant experiences – like inability to start a lawn mower, getting a low score on a test, or losing a game – continued to confirm those subconscious beliefs.

Bottom line, the feelings generated from all of this turned me into an irascible and contentiously drunken ogre, and no one knew why, not even the ogre.

Remember. The most important question we will ever ask God is, "Lord, where is this feeling coming from?"

Your Pain Is Showing!

Never assume *you* know,

"And if anyone thinks that he knows anything, he knows nothing yet as he ought to know."
(1Corinthians 8:2)

Ask the One who knows for sure.

Some overzealous Christians often prattle on, rationalizing their bad behavior toward other men, God and the atmosphere, that they're "okay" – despite monumental shortcomings.

Rather than asking God to show them the source of their dishonesty-driven turmoil, they verbally "explain" it away while they mentally "analyze" their issues. They rationalize the heck out of them.

This is simple, sinful pride in self.

We may be aware of painful circumstances powering negative feelings or beliefs, but only God can pinpoint their origin.

When I finally got around to asking the Lord the $64,000 question around the age of 50, He instantly brought me back to my experience as a nine-year-old boy and in one brief, brilliant moment helped me relive it – this time in a more positive way.

I suddenly recognized much to my shock, and relief, that my feeling of inadequacy was causing my intense and debilitating anger.

My self-loathing, angry attitudes, "me first" mindset and the paranoia I was experiencing all came from one, seemingly insignificant, childhood event. It was misinterpreted, however. A lie.

Once the Lord spoke to that lie and I received His truth about the situation, I never again felt inadequate. I have not experienced another rage-filled moment since that day.

I no longer loathe myself or call myself hateful things. Now I can look into a mirror and feel good about what God made.

If you can't do it, you have a problem only God can help you eliminate.

Chapter Twenty-One
Judging Others

*J*esus warned sternly, we should definitely "judge *not* lest we be judged."

In order for any of us to know, though, firsthand, right from wrong – or truth from lies – we must at times judge the actions of others.

(Note: I am not attempting to defy Scripture, rest assured, only to clarify it).

Be advised that when we judge others for whom they are – or *why* they behave as they do – we tread on some sacred territory.

The Scriptures are clear how we should judge,

"Do not judge according to appearance, but judge with righteous judgment." (John 7:24)

To judge others with righteous judgment means we never consider rumor, gossip or hearsay as truth, nor do we evaluate people or situations solely on circumstantial evidence,

"Consequently; from now on we estimate and regard no one from a [purely] human point of view [in terms of natural standards of value]."
(2Corinthians 5:6a Amplified Bible)

Righteous judgment comes from God alone. As long as we abide in Christ, and carry on constant conversation with Him, we *are* His righteousness – and do indeed know good from evil, pure from vile, holy from unholy.

We must then avoid everything that is not from God, and cling to that which is. Righteous judgment occurs as we respond to the issues and people in our lives by first listening to God and then obeying Him.

Scripture teaches that bad judgment occurs when we base assumptions on the appearance of things or take sides based on info repeated by other people.

When we do this, we step *out* of Christ and face judgment and condemnation ourselves,

"Therefore you are inexcusable, O man, whoever you are who judge, for in whatever you judge another you condemn yourself; for you who judge practice the same things." (Romans 2:1)

Unrighteous judgment arises in those with a guilty conscience. These kinds of folks like to judge something negative or evil in others that is alive and thriving inside them.

This is the worst type of hypocrisy.

When we are in a position to judge others, and we have skeletons in our own dark closets, we divert embarrassing attention, or legal woes, from ourselves by bringing others down.

If we accuse others, we need to look at ourselves first and ask the Lord to reveal what makes us so critical of others.

If the actions of others upset us, causing us to lose our peace, the real problem is in us.

Chapter Twenty-Two
Correcting Others

*M*ost born-again folks would vehemently agree that Almighty God is in charge of the universe – the Main Man, the Big Enchilada, the Head Honcho, Chairman of the Cosmos, Master of Mankind.

Sometimes, though, *we* are in charge – in mere day-to-day earthly matters of course, but God trusts us to handle it all accordingly.

As Christians, He wants us to use our God-given gift of reason and an innate sense of fairness, while acting from the place of peace where we blissfully reside in the bosom of Jesus.

It is important, at those times when we find ourselves in charge of others – or in need of holding them accountable and having a say in deciding their discipline and/or punishment – to do a thorough attitude check.

An unhealthy attitude in this sensitive area of life can clear the way for innumerable difficulties with possibly ruinous results.

Your Pain Is Showing!

Because we are Christians, it is beneficial to keep one question in mind while dealing with situations, and other people, that challenge us to act – be they dangerous, offensive, or just annoying.

Again, we must ask, "*Why* do they offend me and make me feel the way they do?"

Are they hurting our families, friends or us physically or emotionally? Are they breaking a law that may hurt others or themselves?

Do they need someone to show them the error of their ways before they hurt someone? Are they trying but still missing the mark?

Or, are they just rotten to the core? The answers will determine how best to help them.

Therefore, if the actions of anyone stir up in us feelings of fear, anger or disgust, *we* are the first ones in need of assistance.

That statement alone may offend us, or make us angry, defensive or disgusted.

If so, why?

If we attempt to confront and/or help someone who is stirring up bad feelings in us – as well as others – we approach them ready to defend or justify ourselves as though they were the enemy.

They're not, at all.

That particular attitude will only serve to escalate the problem rather than resolve it.

Matthew chapter 23 deals with the manner in which we are to deal with life when we find ourselves offended by others,

> *"Woe to you, scribes and Pharisees, pretenders (hypocrites)! For you clean the outside of the cup and of the plate, but within they are full of extortion (prey, spoil, plunder) and grasping self-indulgence. You blind Pharisee! First clean the inside of the cup and of the plate, so that the outside may be clean also."*
> (Matthew 23:25, 26 Amplified)

Washing off the outside of our cup is not nearly as important as scouring the inside. We may look good from the outside and may think we see others' issues very clearly.

When what we see in others offends or upsets us, it's because the bottom of our own cup contains the silt and debris of leftover misconceptions about our lives. It reminds us of our own skeletons.

When the inside of our cup, our soul, is clean, what we see will not distress us.

The peace of our walk with Jesus allows us to approach others with the compassionate attitude of love, friendship and service rather than an irrational compulsion to correct.

A good microcosmic example is with the students of Teen Challenge, a multidenominational facility for discipleship training – part of a half-century old world-wide Christian organization – where I serve as a teacher and mentor.

For many, before they learn otherwise, the attitude of correcting an offensive brother is more of a cover-up of personal issues – such as addiction, inadequacy, fear, anger or low self-esteem — than a sincere desire to help. They want to divert attention.

When self-protection is the motivation, holding others accountable turns into an act of judgment rather than compassion or mercy.

Cleaning thoroughly the inside of our cups is what Jesus taught in Matthew 7 when He used the analogy of wanting to remove the speck from our brother's eye while not considering the log in our own.

It is God's plan for us to be what I call "qualified spiritual eye surgeons," helping to clear up our brothers and sisters' vision when it becomes clouded with emotional pain.

Being able to see clearly involves much more than just understanding the law.

It is having the proper motivation to operate within it with grace and mercy, which can only come from someone who lives a life of peace, free of fear, frustration and inner pain.

Once we do that, we can hear the truth of God we so desperately need to hear.

Chapter Twenty-Three
Righting Wrong

An ultra-positive, uber-selfless, ultimately world-changing attitude like that of Jesus Christ requires admitting when we are wrong – which is often, and then profoundly.

There is no need, however, to play martyr and, for whatever reason, admit to something we didn't do.

There are also those times when we *are* wrong or could be wrong and times we are simply unsure.

They add up to all the time.

Are we, then, able to admit willingly to the fact, or even the possibility, of being wrong?

If that prospect seems distasteful, then we – of course – need first to ask God to show us why, and help us identify what we believe.

Then He completely erases that potentially discordant track, and makes the correct settings.

Jesus of course was never wrong, yet he never wasted one ounce of energy protecting or defending

Himself. He had infinitely more pressing issues to deal with.

We earthly populace of the material world, on the other hand, spend most of our lives trying to protect ourselves and fend off fear, false accusations, rejection and anything that makes us feel badly.

This is exactly what the enemy (or, what born-again believers call the devil, the world's evil in general) wants us to do. Hence, he keeps on turning up the pressure. Upping the ante. Paying off jurors.

Rather than believing the enemy's lies, we need to view these moments as opportunities to enter even more deeply into God's peace, trust Him to protect, justify – and ultimately exonerate – us when we are falsely accused. And this He will do.

On the other hand, when we try to help someone else who *is* in the wrong without first dealing with the things they trigger in us, the Scripture calls us, in this case, hypocrites. And we are.

If what our brother or sister is doing wrong bothers us, the nagging question is, "If someone is doing something stupid, isn't it natural that it would bother me and others?"

What we really mean, read between the lines, is, "Isn't it acceptable to be upset when others do not act according to my standards?"

The answer is, quite simply, "No."

It is not acceptable for a Christian. It *will* naturally upset others, but that is the point.

We are not your regular natural folks. We are *supernatural* beings because – go ahead, call us crazy – we have God living within us.

Furthermore, as facilitators it is our real, live responsibility to allow God to freely speak the necessary truth to others concerning their steps toward change.

Remember, though, only God can make the inner changes needed to help people conquer their pain.

God's Word, *spoken* by the Holy Spirit, is the only power source that will change another's – or all of our own – attitudes or motivations for life,

"For the word of God is living and powerful, and sharper than any two-edged sword, piercing even to the division of soul and spirit, and of joints and marrow, and is a discerner of the thoughts and intents of the heart." (Hebrews 4:12)

For our part, there is no need to fight to protect ourselves from outside forces trying to hurt or falsely convict us. We may leave it all to God.

We know that the more we try, the more harsh and insurmountable our problems become and the guiltier we seem, as we appear to protest too *much*.

Chapter Twenty-Four
Divinely Human

*O*nce we hear clearly Jesus' wisdom of the ages and firmly commit ourselves to a constant, ongoing conversation with Him, we will enjoy the blessings and strength of God's rest.

Hebrews 4 reveals that when we enter God's rest we have ceased from our human efforts of self protection and self perfection,

"For he who has once entered (God's) rest also has ceased from (the weariness and pain) of human labors, just as God rested from those labors peculiarly His own. Let us therefore be zealous and exert ourselves and strive diligently to enter that rest (of God, to know and experience it for ourselves) that no one may fall or perish by the same kind of unbelief and disobedience (into which those in the wilderness fell)."
(Hebrews 4:10-11 Amplified)

Hebrews refers to God's works of perfect creation – of the earth and all its inhabitants.

There was a time when the Lord Himself finally took His hands off His greatest work, stepped back to look and said, "It is good."

Similarly, we must reach a point in life when we trust God alone and are able to say,

"It is good that God protects me and is maturing me – allowing me sweet peace and preparing me to accomplish His will on this earth and has guaranteed me an eternal stay with Him in paradise."

If we can't ascend to levels of rejuvenating quietude, we'll find ourselves in some trouble.

Scripture calls it outright disobedience and promises, if we don't achieve it, we will "fall," as the Hebrews in the desert did before us.

Based on the number of souls who do not enjoy God's peace, it is clear that it's time to quit accepting indifference, complacence and backsliding as *normal* to Christian growth.

It is disgraceful and disturbing to see the number of Christians who currently fail at this all-important aspect of our walk with Jesus, with a dismissive, "Oh well, what do you expect? Nobody's perfect, and I'm only human!" -type of attitude.

Take note. We are *not* only human!

We are born again, a fact and an act that annihilated our sin nature. Blew it up real good — liberating us from evil!

"...knowing this, that our old man was crucified with Him, that the body of sin might be done away with, that we should no longer be slaves of sin."
(Romans 6:6)

We now have the Spirit of Truth residing within us and working with us outwardly,

"...the Spirit of truth, whom the world cannot receive, because it neither sees Him nor knows Him; but you know Him, for He dwells with you and will be in you." (John 14:17)

This Spirit is the same Spirit who dwelled in, and with, Jesus when He was on earth,

"But you are not in the flesh but in the Spirit, if indeed the Spirit of God dwells in you. Now if anyone does not have the Spirit of Christ, he is not His. And if Christ is in you, the body is dead because of sin, but the Spirit is life because of righteousness. But if the Spirit of Him who raised Jesus from the dead dwells in you, He who raised Christ from the dead will also give life to your mortal bodies through His Spirit who dwells in you." (Romans 8:9-11)

In possessing the Spirit of Jesus Christ, we take on his character and *become* the human version of the righteousness of God – in Him,

"For He made Him who knew no sin to be sin for us, that we might become the righteousness of God in Him." (2Corinthians 5:21)

We have access to the wisdom of the ages,

"If any of you lacks wisdom, let him ask of God, who gives to all liberally and without reproach, and it will be given to him." (James 1:5)

We have obtained the mind of Christ,

"For 'who has known the mind of the Lord that he may instruct Him?' But we have the mind of Christ." (1Corinthians 2:16)

We possess the authority of Heaven,

"Behold, I give you the authority to trample on serpents and scorpions, and over all the power of the enemy, and nothing shall by any means hurt you." (Luke 10:19)

We have been given the use of the Name that is above all names,

"And whatever you ask in My name, that I will do, that the Father may be glorified in the Son. If you ask anything in My name, I will do it." (John 14:13-14)

We have available the full armor of God,

"Put on the whole armor of God, that you may be able to stand against the wiles of the devil. For we do not wrestle against flesh and blood, but against principalities, against powers, against the rulers of the darkness of this age, against spiritual hosts of wickedness in the heavenly places. Therefore take up the whole armor of God, that you may be able to withstand in the evil day, and having done all, to stand. Stand therefore, having girded your waist with truth, having put on the breastplate of righteousness, and having shod your feet with the preparation of the gospel of peace; above all, taking the shield of faith with which you will be able to quench all the fiery darts of the wicked one. And take the helmet of salvation, and the sword of the Spirit, which is the word of God..." (Ephesians 6:11-17)

Finally, God invests divine powers in us,

"For though we walk in the flesh, we do not war according to the flesh. For the weapons of our warfare are not carnal but mighty in God..."
(2Corinthians 10:3-4)

How can we ever say that we are "only" human? To do so is unconscionable and a horrible insult against all Jesus did for us while on earth, and what He stands for today.

It may be tough to swallow, but there is *no excuse* for Christians to fail to allow God to help deal with pain. It's a horrible decision.

We have glorious, complete salvation and a *living* God who, in His love for us, desires to work *with* us, nursing, nurturing and assisting us through *every* moment of life!

Chapter Twenty-Five
Adjusting Attitude

*M*any who vigorously claim Jesus as their Lord would rather have quadruple root canal or swine flu than miss going to church several times a week.

It borders on obsession.

Ask those same Christians how often they verbally speak to God about their daily issues and you will find – surprise, surprise! – the majority of them rarely, if ever, speak aloud to God about *anything*. Some, not even silently.

Christians, just like everyone else, will have all manner of serious relationships with believers, agnostics and non-believers alike – business, personal, intimate and spiritual.

Going to meetings or on dates and talking on the telephone or sending occasional emails or single roses does not build nor nurture relationships of any kind, never mind love.

It takes copious communication and the necessary time to build trusting relationships with anyone in any aspect of our lives.

We cannot fully trust anyone if we don't have a deeply felt, firmly rooted and fervently practiced relationship with him or her.

God is no exception.

Failing to become personal friends with God by communicating with Him and making Him Lord over every decision about every trial of our lives will result in backsliding and failure,

"Let us therefore be diligent to enter that rest, lest anyone fall according to the same example of disobedience." (Hebrews 4:11)

We must know God by experience, which means entering into His rest and enabling ourselves to live in inner peace that surpasses our wildest imagination.

Knowing God through experience helps us make sense out of life.

If we would talk to God about everything during the week, we would have plenty of important ideas to share with others when we do go to church.

And they'd make sense!

Unfortunately, the majority of the current masses of churchgoers drag themselves in for their weekly feeding and pampering, without a thought for anyone else or the inner emotional pain that deprives them of God's friendship and freedom.

This is a defeated church, not a victorious one. The Bible contains some compelling descriptions of how the unequivocal church comes together,

"How is it brethren? Whenever you come together, each of you has a psalm, has a teaching, has a tongue, has a revelation, has an interpretation. Let all things be done for edification." (1Corinthians 14:26), and

"See that no one renders evil for evil to anyone, but always pursue what is good both for yourselves and for all. Rejoice always, pray without ceasing (talk to God about everything), in everything give thanks; for this is the will of God in Christ Jesus for you. Do not quench the Spirit. Do not despise prophecies. Test all things; hold fast what is good. Abstain from every form of evil." (1Thessalonians 5:15-22)

This is church as it should be – filled with mature, enlightened, compassionate, well-informed, service-minded saints of God who know how to walk the walk with Him. They live out of God.

They stroll with Him so smoothly because they consistently communicate out loud with Jesus about everything. When it becomes a habit in a Christian's life, that person continually learns, grows and always has something to share.

It is a sad commentary indeed, when a pastor asks for testimonies and the majority of the body of Christ itself sits silent and fearful.

It is a sure sign of little or lacking spiritual maturity, not to mention limited trust in God.

This is perhaps the most ridiculous and tragic thing of all; they don't yet realize it was Jesus Christ who has provided us with it *all*.

Chapter Twenty-Six
Trusting God

E Pluribus Unum. In God We Trust.

We even print the slogan on our money, which is both fitting and ironic.

Its meaning is, indeed, money in the bank.

Even the most bodacious of Bible-totin', born-again brave hearts, however, needs the occasional attitude check regarding trusting God with *every aspect* of their lives.

Proverbs 3, verses 5 and 6 instruct us to,

"Trust in the Lord with all your heart, and lean not on your own understanding; in all your ways acknowledge Him, and He shall direct your paths."

The word "trust" in the Old Testament means the same as "faith" in the NT.

Therefore, we have faith in the Lord and do not try to figure out or settle in our minds *how* He will do what we need Him to do.

The moment we do, we quit trusting God.

If we are like most lost souls in search of help, we have tried repeatedly to understand ourselves in hopes of improving how we feel about, and live, our earthly lives.

Nevertheless, even if we were to succeed at perfectly understanding why we feel the way we do, we could not change or improve any of our feelings without God's help.

As established earlier, in order to change we need a metamorphosis – change from the inside out – that only God can set in motion.

Remember, until we initiate the exchange with Him, God can't do squat for us.

If we are having trouble trusting Him with our bad situations (it happens to everyone), we ought to be honest about it and tell Him.

If we don't ask for the knowledge, strength and understanding we need, we won't have it,

"You have not because you ask not."
(James 4:2b)

The moment we verbally address God we have expressed our faith in Him and invited Him into our situation, thus *acknowledging* Him in accordance with the instructions of Proverbs 3 verse 6,

"In all your ways acknowledge Him, and He shall direct your paths."

If we need the strength to hang on until the will of God is accomplished, we must ask,

"Therefore do not cast away your confidence, which has great reward. For you have need of endurance, so that after you have done the will of God, you may receive the promise..." (Hebrews 10:35-36)

Many insist, "But I *have* asked for strength and don't feel anything!" My response to that comment is, "What do you want to feel and why do you need to feel anything?"

Receiving from God is an act of faith.

The Bible teaches us that we ought to be living by our faith in God, not by feelings caused by what we see on earth,

"For we walk by faith, not by sight."
(2Corinthians 5:7)

When we ask God for His help, we can count on receiving it because of the promises He has made,

"And whatever you ask in My name, that I will do, that the Father may be glorified in the Son. If you ask anything in My name, I will do it." (John 14:13-14)

If we wish to hear a specific answer from God, we will need to ask Him a *specific* question. It is all right to ask God questions.

As well, should He impart to us something we do not understand, we should tell Him so. God constantly attempts to draw us into deep, intimate discussions that strengthen our relationship with Him.

It is up to us to initiate the conversation and ask the questions that come up, or we will never go deeper into our personal relationship with Him.

Trust is something we all earn. People who expect us to trust them must prove by their actions they deserve it – and vice versa.

If someone we trusted, especially a parent or caregiver, has deceived us, we may find ourselves having a difficult time trusting God.

We shouldn't give up on God just because *people* have failed us, no matter how brutal, cruel or unjust their actions may have been.

God knows well the issues we are facing and He is willing to help us build trust in Him.

In addition, He does not ask us to trust Him in blind faith. He desires us to verbally question and communicate with Him about the issues we face,

"Come now, and let us reason together,' says the Lord." (Isaiah 1:18a)

When we do not properly comprehend how to communicate with Him over the issue of trust, it may help simply to ask Him where the feelings of mistrust come from.

Ask Him to reveal when the deception took place. When He does, simply tell Him what that memory feels like and listen.

This discussion is enough to trigger many people. Most can't believe the extent or intensity of their pain resides within them.

Most erroneously believe that the actions of others are the cause or origin of their pain.

The truth is, no one person truly has the power to make anyone feel *anything*.

Some of our confusion comes from the rationale that if another person has the power to hurt us physically then he or she must also be capable of hurting us emotionally.

We have firmly established that this is patently untrue, practically absurd.

All emotional pain comes from what we believe about ourselves, right? Emotional pain originates from within us and rears its ugly head in behavior, attitude and paradigms.

Those who choose to blame others for their personal issues will never succeed!

Do yourself a favor. Exercise your faith.

Allow your mind to make that small but necessary paradigm shift that will change your life forever, and touch and improve others' in the process.

Trust Him with all your heart and stop attempting to manage your life when left to your own ineffectual earthy human devices,

L. F. Low

"Trust in the Lord with all your heart, and lean not on your own understanding; In all your ways acknowledge Him, and He shall direct your paths."
(Proverbs 3:5-6)

Chapter Twenty-Seven
The Next Step

*O*nce we conquer our pain like gladiators and resolve our issues like Supreme Court judges – and are secure in our personal relationship with our Savior Jesus Christ – we can begin helping others with theirs.

Scripture once again provides instruction and advice for the what, when, and how-to of fulfilling our obligation to help restore others when we notice them hurting or failing,

"Brethren, if a man is overtaken in any trespass, you who are spiritual restore such a one in a spirit of gentleness, considering yourself lest you also be tempted." (Galatians 6:1)

Many Christians might understand this passage to say that if a man is in sin he need only repent and God will restore him. I am not one of them.

Have you ever tried to help someone, attempt to do the right thing, and instead do the wrong thing, ultimately creating an even bigger problem?

We all have! This Scripture passage refers to someone who does not intend to cause problems or break the law, but just seems to miss the mark occasionally.

Repentance does not change their future behavior because they haven't committed a sin of choice. A person in such circumstances needs someone to restore them anyway.

This occurs as a spiritual person, one who has purified their soul by learning how to live in God's peace, facilitates a meeting between the hurting person and God, allowing God to speak to the one missing the easy jump shots.

I have witnessed many good Christians gain freedom over compulsive behaviors for which, unfortunately, the majority of the church would condemn them – if they knew.

These haunted folks, perpetually afraid to seek help because of what they were hearing from the church, are hurting two-fold.

They hear statements like, "If you would quit sinning and do what the Scripture tells you, everything would be fine," or "You are in Christ now; you shouldn't feel the way you feel, and you certainly shouldn't be doing what you do. It's sin, don't do it!"

Overall, I believe the church is sincere in its attempts to help people in pain. They are seriously wrong, though, in their approach and execution – and attitude.

Instead of helping the hurting with the root problems of their lives, it unfortunately condemns, leaving them thinking sin is the root problem.

Their "my way or the highway" paradigm turns people away from Jesus in droves.

It must be remembered, then – judgment and condemnation are often actually the triggered responses of people dealing with, or recovering from, the actions and behaviors of other hurting people.

This is why it is important to understand that other people's actions should not cause us to lose our peace. We've worked too hard to come by it.

Those same feelings also come between us and other people. We must deal with our own lies before we can effectively help others.

No two ways about it.

Bound people are unable to free anyone. Freedom, and then victory, occurs only when a spiritual person facilitates a meeting between the hurting one and the One who can help.

This was Jesus' intent from the beginning.

He wants His hurting, struggling followers to communicate with Him as they receive what only He can give – truth that eradicates vicious lies.

Once having experienced the truth, we are free, suddenly, to choose our own behavior. No longer do we find ourselves pushed into inappropriate or unacceptable actions by our private turmoil and subconscious reactions.

The hundreds of people I have seen restored were all tired of missing the mark. Most felt they were doomed to a lifetime of pain at the hands of compulsive behavior.

Do not be surprised what a lie will cause you to do, succumb to or become.

I have guided hurting people through an alarming array of destructive compulsions and behavior. The following list will help the uninitiated identify some of the most obvious. There are others.

- Alcoholism/Drug Addictions
- Anxieties, Fears, Phobias
- Sexual Perversions
- Abusive/Violent Behavior
- Eating Disorders
- Gambling Addictions
- Spending Compulsions
- Self-Mutilation

Adages like, "Once a drunk always a drunk," or, "A leopard can't change its spots," though, lose their validity when the person involved allows Jesus to restore them, set them free and deliver them from inner pain. Drinking stops. Spots are changed.

I say *when* rather than *if* because eventually everyone hits the bottom of the pit of despair and reaches out for help, myself included.

As Christians, we must be alert and ready to assist when these folks are down and out, asking about Jesus or crying out for help,

"But sanctify the Lord God in your hearts, and always be ready to give a defense to everyone who asks you a reason for the hope that is in you."
(1 Peter 3:15), and

"Brethren, if a man is overtaken in any trespass, you who are spiritual restore such a one in a spirit of gentleness, considering yourself lest you also be tempted." (Galatians 6:1)

Some important thoughts to keep in mind when helping restore/adjust the attitude of those who hurt,

1) This is one of God's special friends. If this person is born-again, he or she is not a sinner but a wounded soldier – someone God loves very much.

This is a brother or sister who wants desperately to stop what they are doing.

If they are not born-again, they are not our enemy but someone for whom Jesus died. They do not wish to be miserable any more than anyone does.

For this reason, we ought to restore them lovingly and gently, considering ourselves lest we also be tempted. None of us is so mature that we cannot fall again. Always consider yourself and your natural weakness and do not get set up for a fall.

Judgment is the first step in that direction, so do not judge or fall to judgment.

2) What did the hurting person do wrong? Are they intentionally, with malice, breaking God's or society's laws?

Is this person trying to be a problem to get attention as a means of getting help? Did they really do something wrong or did they just trigger our own negative stuff?

3) What would Jesus do? He would always check with His Heavenly Father to determine what He should do and then obey,

"Then Jesus answered and said to them, 'Most assuredly, I say to you, the Son can do nothing of Himself, but what He sees the Father do; for whatever He does, the Son also does in like manner.'"
(John 5:19)

We are always to do what Jesus would do, recognizing that anything we ask from the Father, within the context of following Him, He will most certainly do for us,

"And whatever you ask in My name (conformable to my character and my purpose), *that I will do, that the Father may be glorified in the Son. If you ask anything in my name* (conformable to my character and my purpose), *I will do it."* (John 14:13-14 Authors notes added for clarity)

Then, our lives generate glory to our God.

Chapter Twenty-Eight
Fear Of Confrontation

*I*s fear a sin?

It certainly deters us from confronting others in need of direction or requiring correction. It makes us lax in restoring or leading others to the grace of God.

In John 14, verse 27, Jesus himself warned us, emphatically at that,

"Do not let your heart be troubled, neither let it be afraid."

Scripture also teaches that Jesus' perfect love casts out all fear and that God did not create us with a spirit of fear,

"There is no fear in love, but perfect love casts out fear because fear involves torment. But he who fears has not been made perfect in love." (1John 4:18), and

"For God has not given us a spirit of fear, but of power and of love and of a sound mind."
(2Timothy 1:7)

Allowing fear to incapacitate us will make us miserable, as do all forms of disobedience. We all know the wages of not obeying God.

All of that said, it is safe to say that yes, fear can be a sinful emotion that should be put down like the voracious evil beast that often rages in our loins.

In all cases, God is with us!

The next obvious question is how we rid ourselves of fear of confronting people whose pain is causing them to act out defiantly – something that happens frequently in my mentoring the folks at Teen Challenge of the Midlands.

I try to point out that they ought to look at their dire situation as a perfect opportunity to serve their troubled brothers or sisters by maybe helping them grow past their anger.

If we are angry or upset with the people we are supposed to be serving, things will not end well and will drive us to protect ourselves, not to serve them.

However, if we first work with God to eliminate our reason for being upset, we remove the log from our eyes and see more clearly the way to help others grow and learn from their own mistakes.

The contention and/or conflict caused by trying to take specks out of others' eyes with a railroad tie in our own is what keeps the body of Christ weak and ineffective.

After all, Christianity means "like Christ." Either we are or we are not.

Which is it?

In my ministry I witness too many parents, spouses and church and business leaders who refuse to hold their partners, children, staff, or associates (thus themselves) accountable by confronting them when wrong.

Leaders don't behave this way. They must always confront insubordination in the ranks, as well as incompetence and corrupt motives.

Without an immediate correction of those in error, the safety of the entire group could end up in peril. They are unprotected.

We must protect others from wrongdoers and the wrongdoers from themselves,

"Son of man, I have made you a watchman for the house of Israel; therefore hear a word from My mouth, and give them warning from Me; When I say to the wicked, 'You shall surely die,' and you give him no warning, nor speak to warn the wicked from his wicked way, to save his life, that same wicked man shall die in his iniquity; but his blood I will require at your hand." (Ezekiel 3:17-18)

Additionally, we can be the ones who keep someone from a tremendous failure or a fatal mistake – a situation that, more often than not, turns into a life-long friendship.

Take heed. It's easy to say, "I told you so," or, "I knew that would happen," after the person has failed or hurt themselves or others.

This is the coward's way.

Ours is the Christian way.

The man or woman of God, who loves others as He does, will confront them when they are in error.

Chapter Twenty-Nine
Dealing With Anger

*A*nger in itself is not sin.

However, what we choose to do with it and how we respond to others while under its influence can be.

Countless Christians, ironically, have a difficult time dealing with anger. Many of them believe anger is a sin and hate to admit how they really feel. However, Scripture teaches that anger is not sin but how we respond could be sinful,

"Be angry and do not sin: Do not let the sun go down on your wrath." (Ephesians 4:26)

If we allow ourselves to fly into a vicious fit of rage, or express our wrath physically or verbally in a dangerously destructive manner, our response is a sin.

To hold on to fury without expressing it, and mentally stash those nagging negative feelings in a dark and miserable storeroom in the back of your mind, is also a sin.

People who do this like to call their anger "hurt feelings." They find it hard to deal with these feelings, the other people that may have caused them, and the situations triggering their anger.

Storing up these hurt feelings causes us to take offense, and we miss the opportunity to walk in God's love. Doing so will also eventually result in the disintegration, and possible destruction, of our faith,

> *"For in Christ Jesus neither circumcision nor uncircumcision avails anything, but faith working through love."* (Galatians 5: 6)

Taking offense, internalizing anger, incites rejection of others, splits churches, families, and friends. It causes many to walk away from their God-given call and ultimately, like Esau, their spiritual inheritance.

People who internalize excessive anger will ultimately explode in a manic spasm of vitriol when they can no longer suppress it – having spent weeks, or even years, wallowing in self pity and justifying anger as hurt feelings.

Anger is the fruit of fear – a powerful secondary emotion intended to protect us from our inner pain.

Un-checked anger and rampant inner pain causes our reprehensible attitudes and/or hate paradigms to proliferate and overpower us.

Fear comes when we believe we are about to lose irrevocably something of serious value, become publicly exposed, or found to be defenseless and out of control, like the plight of the addict.

For many years, I suffered from extreme feelings of inadequacy. When these feelings were triggered, in an attempt to regain control, I would become incensed, burying my true feelings under frenetic fits of fury and exhibitions of anger.

Fearfulness and rage were the only "fruits" of life, while crippling feelings of inadequacy and the memories that produced them were the "root" cause.

Had I continued to ignore or internalize the anger, I'd have never experienced freedom from the feelings of inadequacy plaguing me.

Internalized rage is destructive because it gives bitterness and vengeful feelings control.

These feelings are what Matthew 18; verse 34 refers to when it speaks of the "torturers,"

"And his master was angry, and delivered him to the torturers until he should pay all that was due to him."

The torturers can be demonic presences, given access to our minds through resentment and hostility. We may find it difficult believing Christians can be host to demonic activity. Nevertheless, it is possible.

Evil spirits reside in the lies of the mind.

Throughout our years of helping hundreds of people resolve their persistent anger, we've seen a few cases of demonic oppression.

Skeptical? Okay.

But be cautious not to deny the existence of that with which you have no experience. This could leave you vulnerable and make you the enemies' target in the future. Don't be a sitting duck.

Remain teachable and ready to receive new revelation from the Lord, always testing the viability of the earthly matters we face by asking Him to verify or reject them for you.

This will keep you safe.

Instead, we will find ourselves constantly tormented by those who have hurt and offended us every time we trigger those memories and their associated feelings.

"Peace I leave with you, My peace I give to you; not as the world gives do I give to you. Let not your heart be troubled, neither let it be afraid." (John 14:27)

Chapter Thirty
Forgiveness From The Heart

Many in the body of Christ may have experienced serious injury through repeated sexual, physical or emotional abuse – often at the hands of so-called loved ones.

For them, forgiving the ones who have committed such profound and heinous sins against them is a difficult concept to grasp.

One reason for this, in my view, is that the church has done a less than adequate job of teaching the principles of forgiveness.

The following are a few simple, scripturally sound comments concerning forgiveness.

Forgiveness is not:

1) Denial we suffered an injustice.

2) Silence about the injustice we suffered.

3) Suppression of righteous anger.

4) Rejection of desire for/right to, justice.

5) Pardon for those who sinned against us.
6) Reconciliation, except as a talking point.
7) Weakened defense from future wrong.

Forgiveness is:
1) Trust in God.
2) Disconnection from the offender.
3) Willingness to redirect the offense onto God so He can deal with the offender, and protect them and us from future occurrences,

"If you forgive (release or loose) *the sins of any, they are forgiven them; if you retain* (bind or hold) *the sins of any, they are retained."*
(John 20:23; author's comment)

When we refuse to forgive, we bind the offender to the offense and emotionally hold them to ourselves. This makes God unable to deal with the one who hurt us.

Refusing to forgive means, we have chosen to usurp God of His place as Righteous Judge. He will remain unable to seek justice for us until we have released the event and the offender to Him.

Releasing the offender by offering them forgiveness has nothing to do with their guilt or innocence. It is up to God to decide that,

"Beloved, do not avenge yourselves, but rather give place to wrath; for it is written, 'vengeance is Mine, I will repay,' says the Lord.'" (Romans 12:19)

Those offended or sinned-against are only responsible to release the offender and his or her sin to God, so He can affect justice and reconciliation on their behalf.

Three Scriptures dealing with the need to forgive those who offended or hurt us follow,

"Then Peter came to Him and said, 'Lord, how often shall my brother sin against me, and I forgive him? Up to seven times?' Jesus said to him, 'I do not say to you, up to seven times, but up to seventy times seven...'" (Matthew 18:21-22)

"Then his master, after he had called him, said to him, 'You wicked servant! I forgave you all that debt because you begged me. Should you not also have had compassion on your fellow servant, just as I had pity on you?' And his master was angry, and delivered him to the torturers until he should pay all that was due to him. So My heavenly Father also will do to you if each of you, from his heart, does not forgive his brother his trespasses." (Matthew 18:32-35), and

"And whenever you stand praying, if you have anything against anyone, forgive him that your Father in heaven may also forgive you your trespasses. But if you do not forgive, neither will your Father in heaven forgive your trespass." (Mark 11:25-26)

On our journey toward Jesus' perfect peace, it is vitally important to properly deal with anger.

When it seems impossible to obtain Jesus' promised peace, it's because our memory consists of, among innumerable emotions of varying intensity including, yep, anger.

Most people forgive to the degree they are personally capable of and manage to deal with their anger cognitively, therefore consistently.

But that just is not enough.

They are unable to forgive from the heart. Jesus, however, explains how to make it possible,

"So My heavenly Father also will do to you if each of you, from his heart, does not forgive his brother his trespasses." (Matthew 18: 35*)*

Forgiveness from the heart for real is accomplished by forgiving the offense while returning to the memory during which the offense occurred.

Jesus' perfect inner peace will elude us as long as our memories are fraught with anger, bitterness, hatred, jealously or revenge. All of these emotions work right against us.

Your Pain Is Showing!

As effective Christians, our hearts, minds and souls must become as pure as His.

That happens as we allow the Lord to reveal the origin of the anger we have left and let Him lend power to accomplish the task.

Then we can forgive from the heart.

Conclusion

*T*oo many Christians work with God on a few issues and receive some great peace. Then they expect never again to have any bad feelings, disappointments or problems.

Our struggles never end while on earth.

The hardened, haphazard world in which we live constantly challenges and attempts to change us. The ever-increasing stresses of secular society, our jobs and our own family relationships continue to exert pressure on us.

It is a time when we born-again believers experience seemingly insurmountable barriers to doing what Jesus would do. Knowing how to speak to God is more important than ever.

Christianity is not about living *for* God but about allowing God to live *through* you!

As we earnestly invite God to live *in* us, we are actually living out of God or from the overflow of our relationship with Him.

I will say it *one* more time – the most important thing any of God's creatures can do is learn to communicate effectively with Him.

In the process we develop a relationship with Him. As with any relationship, time and effort are required to develop and nurture it.

That is why Scriptures instruct us to pray continuously or, talk to God about everything.

Our Heavenly Father invited us into the most intimate of relationships when he said,

"Cast all your cares upon Me, because I care for you." (1Peter 5:7)

He is saying, "When you feel bad, tell Me."

Therefore, do not lose heart if struggles continue to come your way.

Rather, rejoice!

They all serve as doorways to God so we learn from, and mature in Him, and produce a laudable life of righteousness,

"And the effect of righteousness will be peace [internal and external], and the result of righteousness will be quietness and confident trust forever." (Isaiah 32:17 Amplified)

Remember we are all on an extended, extensive and endlessly long journey. So, treat life as a marathon, not a dash.

When we finish it doesn't matter; running strong – pain-free in God's grace – does.

Run steady. Move forward toward God.

Appendix One
Pinpointing Pain

*T*he following is a series of eight simple steps which will greatly help in the process of communicating and real sharing of thoughts, feelings and problems – with God.

Throughout these steps, it will also be evident how to receive truth from Him; making possible the elimination of the lies that cause pain.

Step 1: Know what you feel.

We cannot receive help until we are able to admit freely our need for it. We do not need to label the feeling, only to recognize we are not living in peace and need assistance.

We Christians have ignored our feelings for far too long! Heaven forbid we slip up and admit how we *really* feel – for fear that any horrible or humiliating confession would just compound our problems.

Truth is, God gave us emotions so we'd know when something is wrong in our soul.

If we have a severe stomach pain, which flares up every time we eat, you do not ignore it. We consult a doctor immediately, as pain means something is terribly wrong.

Ignoring such symptoms results in death.

Your Pain Is Showing!

It is also important to attend quickly to the painful emotions that we occasionally – or constantly – experience because they, too, indicate something just as deadly within us!

Just as physical pain weakens and ravages our bodies, emotional pain strikes a different kind of agony, and great misapprehension, in our hearts. It also ravages us physically.

Emotions are nerve endings of the soul.

Emotional pain or negative feelings come from the same lies, and the lies come from the misinterpretation of our experience. Catch 22.

A record of our experience resides within, in memories, and each has three aspects:

a) The mental picture of the experience.
b) The emotion, or how it felt at the time.
c) The interpretation of the experience.

If, because of generational influences or simple insufficient understanding of others' intentions, we misinterpret an experience, we automatically ingest a lie that will continue to poison us until uprooted and removed.

A lie believed to be true infects our soul and our will, as the physical pain from a deep bruise continues to bring the same emotional pain when bumped.

Our lovely Jesus, in John 8, verse 32 spoke of the remedy to this situation,[14]

"And you shall know (or experience) *the truth, and the truth shall make you free."* and, *"Therefore if the Son makes you free, you shall be free indeed."*

Scripture says faith, not need, moves God,

"But without faith it is impossible to please Him, for he who comes to God must believe that He is, and that He is a rewarder of those who diligently seek Him." (Hebrews 11:6)

Therefore, if we are not willing to admit we feel horribly and humble ourselves by asking for His help, there is no way of seeking nor obtaining lasting freedom from wounded pasts, or completely renewing our minds.

Locating the memory that caused the pain is quite simple. Ask God where it is.

Step 2: <u>Vocally ask Jesus where the bad feeling comes from.</u>

Everything we say and do (or the "fruit" of our lives) is a result of emotion. Subconscious

---

[14] Commentary by author.

mental activity produces it. Subconscious mental activity powers 98 per cent of every action we take or word we speak.

Positive and pure feelings promote good fruit, while bad feelings produce negative fruit. It is useless to criticize the wretched fruit of a person's life unless we have a proven successful method of changing it.

The only way to improve the fruit of our lives is to heal the diseased roots of issues causing it to decay.

Only Jesus, through the Holy Spirit, can show us the existing, cancerous root-rot of anything in our past. He never fails and He is always acutely accurate.

Be sure to ask Him verbally! Don't just think it. Scriptures are clear that we have not because we ask not, not because we think not.

Step 3: Expect to receive a memory.

Remember, Jesus cannot move because of need alone. Our faith frees God to move for us. If we do not *expect* to receive anything, we will get nothing!

Put your faith to work by expecting God to help you. In my ministry, I witness Him help, with perfect accuracy, everyone who comes seeking His help and who've given up trying to help themselves.

A word of caution: don't make the mistake of assuming *you* know where the memory is.

Allow Jesus to show you to make sure you have accessed the root cause of your pain. The memory you have may only be a secondary memory that merely confirms the pain created by an earlier experience.

When you see or recall the root memory, put your faith to work by trusting in the Lord with all your heart. Above all, do *not* rely on your limited understanding.

Step 4: <u>Ask yourself what feels true about *you* in this memory.</u>

Identifying what feels true about us in the memory Jesus reveals is how we discover the lie we believe to be true. This is the root source of our pain.

If what feels true is not obvious then ask Jesus to tell you what you believe to be true about the experience He has shown you.

Allow Him to help pinpoint the lie.

Step 5: <u>Tell *Jesus* what feels true about you in the memory.</u>

There is no need to ramble on in your explanation, nor is it necessary to try to justify or protect your actions.

Jesus knows exactly what happened and why. He does not need to hear it ad absurdum. He merely needs you to admit what feels true in that particular memory.

If you feel worthless simply say, "Jesus, I feel worthless in this memory."

Tell Him what you feel in as few words as possible and then be *still* so you can receive the truth from Him. Allow Him to respond to your feeling,

> *"Be still, and know that I am God."*
> (Psalm 46:10a)

Step 6: <u>Expect to hear the truth from Jesus.</u>

In order to raise your confidence in the expectation of receiving answers to your problems from Him, look at these Scriptures of encouragement,

"Call to me, and I will answer you, and show you great and mighty things, which you do not know," (Jeremiah 33:3)

"However, when He, the Spirit of truth, has come, He will guide you into all truth; for He will not speak on His own authority, but whatever He hears He will speak and He will tell you things to come." (John 16:13) and,

"But let him ask in faith, with no doubting, for he who doubts is like a wave of the sea driven and tossed by the wind. For let not that man suppose that he will receive anything from the Lord; he is a double-minded man, unstable in all his ways." (James 1:6-8)

As the Lord speaks, it comes as a gentle sense of "just knowing" – knowledge that is not the product of our human thinking. Sometimes God speaks through memory pictures or remembrances.

How He communicates with you is up to Him, but one thing you can know for sure. He *will* respond to your pain, even as you struggle to stay focused on what He shows you, and cling to the perilous attitudes within.

If you find yourself unable to receive the truth from Jesus, ask yourself, "Do I feel anger in this memory?" If anger and vengeance are present, they need your undivided attention before you can move on.

If you detect anger, go to Step 1 in Appendix Two following. After you release the anger, come back and re-test the memory by beginning again at Step 4 and following through to Step 8.

Step 7: <u>Speak aloud what you sense Jesus has said to you.</u>

As mentioned in Step 6, God may very well show you something by use of a mental picture. If He does, speak out what the picture is telling you.

This step is vitally important. To be totally released from the lie you must speak aloud what the Lord is saying.

Why? Look at Isaiah 55, verse 11,

"So shall My word be that goes forth from My mouth; It shall not return to Me void, But it shall accomplish what I please, And it shall prosper in the thing for which I sent it."

The Word of the Lord must return to Him in order to accomplish what He sent it to do. His Word returns to Him as we speak it.

Only then will it accomplish the mission, for which He sent it,

"For out of the abundance of the heart the mouth speaks." (Matthew 12:343b)

We only speak what we believe in, or know to be true – that in which we have faith. When we speak the words God has spoken to us, we are adding our faith to His Word and sending it back to Him.

Then it accomplishes the thing He sent it forth to do – make us free!

Step 8: Ask Him if there are any more memories that could cause this pain.

If He shows you another memory return to Step 4 and work it as you did the last one.

If there are no other memories, you will have a revelation that will settle in your heart to inform you that it is finished.

You'll be filled with joy, and get a sense of what it's *really* like to feel relaxed and relieved.

I have seen the most hardened cynic feel it.

Appendix Two
Finding Forgiveness

*I*n the thousands of hours my wife Dixie and I have spent helping people find inner peace, we have found the following four steps to be extremely effective.

Step 1: <u>Allow Jesus to show you the root memory or origin of your anger.</u>

If you have come to this section because you found anger or other revengeful feelings in the root memory of an emotion, go on to Step 2 below.

If you are dealing with anger as the fruit of your life, follow the eight steps in Appendix One first, in order to determine which feeling is actually causing your anger.

Step 2: <u>Ask Jesus for His power and ability to forgive the offender.</u>

Jesus Himself could not forgive the sins that crucified Him without the power of His Father – neither can we. For this reason, do not let pride take you. Ask Jesus to help you.

One of many ploys of the enemy is to make you feel you have already forgiven someone who has trespassed against you, and that this is a wasted step.

It is not.

As has been established, if you have *any* revengeful feelings in the memory you are dealing with, you have only dealt with it cognitively. This won't cut it.

Do not allow the enemy or your own mind to deceive you. While remaining focused on the memory, say,

Jesus, I know I need to forgive _____, but right now I cannot do it alone. Would you please help me?

Once you have asked for His help, stay focused on the memory and its feeling. You will know you have had the Lord's help when you suddenly feel forgiving is do-able.

It is as if the presence of the Lord comes alongside of you in the memory. Suddenly, you *know* you can do it.

Step 3: Forgive and release the offender using the following pattern.

Jesus, I thank you for your help and I choose to forgive _____ because I believe that (he/she/they) did not have a clue how badly they hurt me. Therefore, I give _____ to you, and ask you to please take this anger and bitterness from me, and heal me.

Your Pain Is Showing!

Exercise caution here because the enemy does not want you to forgive anyone.

At this point, you may feel strongly that the offender *did* in fact know exactly what he or she was doing. Not only that, you may be convinced they knew how deeply it hurt you.

At the risk of seeming to defend your offender, consider the following.

First, none of us fully understand exactly how the things we say or do effect eternity. If we did, we most likely would not do them – or perhaps we'd lose our minds.

And then, our offender honestly may not know he/she has hurt us. Stranger things have happened, and things are not always about us.

Finally, assuming for the moment that they *did* know what they were doing, we must follow the pattern cut by Jesus if we are truly to forgive from the heart.

Remember, it was impossible to do alone. His Holy Father had His back. Look closely at 1Peter 2, verse 18 to 23,

"[You who are] household servants, be submissive to your master with all [proper] respect, not only to those who are kind and considerate and reasonable, but also to those who are surly (overbearing, unjust, and crooked). For one is regarded favorably (is

approved, acceptable, and thankworthy) if, as in the sight of God, he endures the pain of unjust suffering. [After all] what kind of glory [is there in it] if when you do wrong and are punished for it, you take it patiently? But if you bear patiently with suffering [which results] when you do right and that is undeserved, it is acceptable and pleasing to God. For even to this were you called [it is inseparable from your vocation]. For Christ also suffered for you, leaving you [His personal] example, so that you should follow in His footsteps. He was guilty of no sin, neither was deceit (guile) ever found on His lips. When He was reviled and insulted, He did not revile or offer insult in return; [when] He was abused and suffered, He made no threats [of vengeance]; but he trusted [Himself and everything] to Him Who judges fairly."
(Amplified)

This Scripture deals with suffering at the hands of an offender, accusation of things you did not do and punishment for what you are not responsible.

Look specifically at verse 21,

"For even to this were you called [it is inseparable from your vocation]. For Christ also suffered for you, leaving you [His personal] example, so that you should follow in His footsteps." (Amplified)

Another Scripture regarding how to follow Jesus is 1John 2, verse 6,

"Whoever says he abides in Him ought [as a personal debt] to walk and conduct himself in the same way in which He walked and conducted Himself." (Amplified)

We are to intentionally follow Jesus' footsteps, which means His *example*. His is the only way of living that works.

The enemy and your own human mind will do everything possible to talk you out of it.

Do not let that happen.

Allow the Holy Spirit to help you through and follow these time-tested, proven steps.

You will be glad you did, or you will be terribly sorry you did not – should you allow your mind to talk you into saying, "This is just too hard," or, "It just isn't fair."

We are not talking about fairness. Nobody ever said that life was going to be fair. We are talking about something much bigger; finding perfect inner peace, now and forever.

I witness people who heretofore have persisted valiantly through their pain, instantly released from it. Previous to that, it is clearly visible on their faces and in their posture. Their whole body language screams pain.

Within seconds the feeling of freedom, as the burden lifts off them, is palpable in the room. The release is so profound that normally a gusty sigh of relief is emitted.

I am convinced you will literally *feel* the pain lifting away. Therefore, I am completely confident in saying, should you not feel anything, you are likely still grasping some stubborn part of your anger and not actually forgiving from the heart.

Try again and stay focused on the memory the Lord is showing you. Don't give up!

Step 4: Thank Jesus for the release and ask if there is anything else causing your anger.

If the Lord shows you a new memory, return to Step 2 and work it again. And again.
And again. Amen

Appendix Three
Testimonies

*T*he following testimonies are from a few of my latest students at Teen Challenge of the Midlands, [15] who volunteered to share their hearts in hopes they could help others who may be fighting the same or similar battles.

They also offered to give testimony of God's grace; thanking Him for the instant release from years of pain. The same peace is available for all who will approach Him and learn to communicate with Him.

Drug Deadened To Alive In Peace

"I was born in a small town in the midwest plains. I had a normal small town childhood. By 17 I was a full blown, needle-in-the-arm meth addict. At 18 I hooked up with a violent biker gang and started running dope for them. As my life spiraled out of control, jails and rehabs seemed to be a never ending cycle. At 28, doctors told me that if I continued to drink the way I was I would not see 30. Unfortunately that didn't faze me – something deeper inside was pushing me that

---

[15] Teen Challenge of the Midlands is located in Colfax Iowa. Details online at www.tcmid.org. Pastor Low's business information, ministry details and publication history at www.LarryLow.com

overpowered any fear of death. After a period of homelessness I found and entered Teen Challenge. God saved my life through this program. I was taught how to speak to God as a way to deal with all my inner pain. Through my communication with God, He instantly took all my pain and with it the urges to use and drink. He continues to change and strengthen me daily as we continue our relationship. The greatest thing is all I have to do is ask Him. I honestly believe that without this program, what I have learned here and God's love I would be dead by now."

K.V.
Nebraska

Tourette's, Panic Attacks Defeated

"Before I entered Teen Challenge I would run from any type of emotional pain. All of this pain was caused by lies I believed about myself. I had regular panic attacks and was diagnosed with and treated for Tourette's syndrome. The doctors said it was because of a chemical imbalance in my head. The thing is, though, the medication never really helped me. I have tried just about every SSRI (Selective Serotonin Reuptake Inhibitor) and antidepressant known, but I still made my noise every five minutes or so as well as my panic attacks continued. In order to deal with my issues I started gambling and became a compulsive gambler. When I entered the TC program, they showed me how to deal with my inner pain. Any time I feel uneasy, upset or angry I speak to God and ask Him why I feel this way and allow Him to speak to me. Through my communication with God and listening to the Holy Spirit, my life has become so much more peaceful. I no longer feel the need to gamble. The Lord has healed my Tourette's that I lived with for over 20 years by showing me a memory of when I was five years old and giving me the truth about that day. From that day on I have not displayed the Tourette's symptoms outwardly. I am now merely breaking the habits established from living life with inner pain for so long. And, I do not have panic attacks any longer. I now live free!"

D.V.
Nebraska

From Abuse To Love And Peace

"I grew up with a loving mother, a loving sister and an abusive father. I was abused mentally and physically, reaching points of being hospitalized for head traumas. I was introduced to marijuana at 11 years old. Pot took all the anger and hate I felt away from me, or so I thought. As the abuse continued, my anger grew stronger and stronger to the point where weed didn't work anymore. I resorted to partying, fighting, and doing a lot of different drugs just trying to escape my hatred. In eight years I went from a little boy who smoked a little weed to deal with an abusive father, to an everyday stealing, scamming, and fighting heroin addict. On July 13 I overdosed on heroin. My heart beat was four beats per minute. By the grace of God He spared me and brought me to Teen Challenge of the Midlands. During my first week there I learned how to speak to God and how to hear from Him. When I talked to Him about all my pain and anger my eyes suddenly began to run with tears and my body felt lighter than a feather. All of my anger and hate simply vanished and all I had to do was to ask Him. I have learned to communicate with God and I have never been happier. The power of God has taught me to forgive my father. My dad and I have a real relationship now. The best part is when he says he loves me and is proud of me. I know for a fact that if it wasn't for God, I would not have nor want my dad in my life. I thank God everyday for changing my life and showing me that I am loved. God gives life; all we must do is surrender to His love and talk to Him – really, just talk to Him."

Z. A.
Illinois

Your Pain Is Showing!

Reference
Bibliography

New King James Version of the Holy Bible. Copyright ©1979, 1980, 1982 by Thomas Nelson, Inc.

The Amplified Bible, Copyright © by the Zondervan Corporation 1962, 1964, 1965, 1977, 1986.

The Amplified New Testament, Copyright ©1958, 1987.

The Amplified Gospel of John, Copyright ©1954, 1987 By The Lockman Foundation, La Habra, CA 90631.

The Hebrew-Greek Key Study Bible, Authorized King James Version, Zodhiates' original and complete system of Bible study. Compiled and Edited by Spiros Zodhiates,

Th.D.Copyright ©1984 by Spiros Zodhiates and AMG International, Inc., D/B/A AMG Publishers, Chattanooga, TN 37422.

Holy Bible, New International Version®, NIV®. Copyright ©1973, 1978, 1984 International Bible Society.
Used by permission of Zondervan Publishing House. All rights reserved.

"NIV"/"New International Version" are trademarks registered in the United States Patent and Trademark Office by International Bible Society. Used by the permission of the International Bible Society.

The Biology Of Belief, By Dr. Bruce H. Lipton, Ph. D. Copyright ©2005, by Bruce Lipton. Published by Mountain of Love/Elite Books, Santa Rosa, CA 95404.

Great Attitudes, by Charles Swindoll.
Copyright ©2006, by Charles Swindoll. Published by Thomas Nelson. Quote available at www.bigeye.com/attitude.htm.

Teen Challenge of the Midlands
900 N. League Road
P.O. Box 185
Colfax, IA 50054
www.tcmid.org.

Key Words And Phrases

A
absolute freedom, 2, 7
abundant life, 7
Anger, 82, 184, 185, 200
aptitude, 13
Aptitude, 15
aptitude is, 15
attitude, 11, 12, 13, 15, 16, 24, 26, 27, 31, 33, 34, 36, 39, 43, 47, 60, 61, 67, 68, 84, 94, 97, 100, 118, 119, 120, 131, 150, 151, 152, 156, 167, 177
Attitude is, 12, 13
B
browbeat, 125
butterfly, 46
C
carnal-minded, 92
Christianity, 7, 27, 114, 122, 127, 181
Cleaning the outside of our cup, 152
cognitive, 21, 23, 26, 29, 33, 46
communication, 37, 84, 164
consciously, 23, 25
cope, 32
coping mechanism, 28
D
deceiving yourself, 81
déjà Vu moment, 22
deliverance, 35, 110
depression, 26, 79, 103

destiny, 3
drug rehabilitation, 33

E

Emotional pain, 83, 171, 195
emotional pains, 34
emotions, 24, 40, 41, 43, 82, 92, 184, 194, 195
evil, 109, 110, 148, 161, 165, 185
experience, 4, 20, 21, 22, 23, 24, 27, 29, 60, 84, 99, 104, 143, 145, 157, 164, 186, 195, 196, 198
experiencing God, 7
experiential memory, 21, 28, 46

F

fellowship of His sufferings, 59
flashbacks, 22
freedom, xi, 3, 19, 54, 70, 135, 164, 174, 185, 196, 208

G

gentle knowing, 51
God's rest, 157
good eye, 81

H

hobbyist Christians, 7
homosexual, 135
Hypnosis, 34
hypocrisy, 123

I

in due time, 89, 99
inadequacy, 25, 122, 135, 143, 145, 152, 185
intellectually, 23
interpretation, 17, 144, 165, 195
interpretations, 17, 21
interprets, 20

J
joie de vivre, 27
just get over it, 35
K
know, 19, 29, 58, 62, 74, 82, 98, 103, 110, 111, 112, 122, 145, 157, 159, 165, 196, 198, 199, 200, 204, 205
L
lesbian, 135
live out of God, 6
M
memorize, 46
memory picture, 23
metamorphosis, 168
metamorphous, 46
missed the mark, 107
N
nerve-endings, 31
New Covenant, 66
O
obedience, 2, 30, 60, 65, 72, 73, 115
open door policy, 74
P
pain motivated behaviors, 36
paranoia, 78, 145
Paranoia, 24
patience, 16, 24, 27, 62, 98
peace, 6, 2, 19, 32, 63, 73, 74, 92, 93, 116, 138, 149, 153, 161, 164, 175, 186, 190, 192, 193, 194, 207
penal system, 33
protecting self, 20

psychological conflicts, 65
psychology, 5, 43, 47
purifying your soul, 114, 116
purpose, 4, 27, 39, 82, 131

R

receptors, 20
rehabilitation, 43
reprogram, 17
Restoration Ministry Training, 136
root memory, 198, 203

S

sanctification by truth, 63, 116
self condemnation, 3
Self-absorbed people, 70
self-destruction, 15, 143
self-improvement, 26
self-protection, 153
shake it off, 35
sin, 29, 30, 34, 58, 59, 60, 61, 62, 75, 92, 110, 111, 158, 159, 160, 173, 183, 189, 206
spirit of the mind, 42
Spirit-minded, 92
spiritual maturity, 62
Strongholds, 65
subconscious, 17, 21, 23, 24, 28, 31, 46, 47, 144, 175, 197
subconscious memory, 46
subconsciously, 16, 20, 23
super-computer, 17, 21, 22

T

tolerance, 16
transformation, 35, 42, 44, 47, 57, 66

trauma, 5
truth, 4, 16, 17, 19, 28, 29, 30, 35, 40, 42, 47, 48, 49, 56, 63, 75, 80, 81, 82, 83, 88, 92, 105, 116, 117, 121, 132, 135, 143, 144, 146, 147, 152, 153, 156, 159, 161, 171, 175, 194, 196, 199, 200

W

way, the truth and the life, 19
what feels true, 198, 199
witnesses, 4, 5
women's work, 127
word of truth, 27

About The Author

After a dramatic encounter with Jesus Christ in 1982, Larry Low began preaching the Gospel and serving the Lord as signs and miracles abounded.

Immediately following his encounter with Jesus, the Holy Spirit enrolled him in His University. For several years, the Holy Spirit would get him up at 4 am and teach him the Word of God until 6 am.

That personalized training and the necessary, faithful communication with Lord God helped him understand that Jesus wants a personal, intimate relationship with his children. He recognized the call of God on his life to serve Him in ministry. However, it took nine years before full time ministry replaced his career in the computer industry.

From the very beginning of his walk with God, Brother Low's passion has been to know Jesus Christ personally. He has wanted nothing more since that day he met Jesus and the Holy Spirit. Since that first meeting Brother Low has personally witnessed the results of immediately obeying the voice of the Holy Spirit.

In addition to serving as pastor since 1984, he has traveled and ministered in pastor's conventions and to local churches throughout the United States, Philippines, Haiti, Mexico and South East Asia. He continues to travel and minister, holding "Responding to the Cry of Our Culture" seminars as doors and hearts open to him.

Brother Low is the founder and current president of Zoë Ministries and Master's Touch. He calls people out of spiritual apathy by teaching the Body how easy it is to hear the voice of God and how quickly Jesus responds to their concerns and fears.

His goal is to help the Body step up to a higher walk with God through a lifestyle of genuine Christianity. His prayer is that church leaders begin to recognize the pain that surrounds them as an opportunity, awaiting them and their churches.

Larry Low's greatest joy in ministry is to see the spiritually dead come alive in Christ as they experience how easy it is to gain His inner peace in their life. When spiritually lifeless persons experience the joy of abiding in Christ for the first time, revival begins.

In his mind, *nothing* is better than that.

About The Editor

*D*aryl Jung holds a bachelor's degree from York University in Toronto, Canada, and a Master of Arts degree from the University of Iowa, USA, both in English. He was a founding staffer and 20-year-veteran associate editor of NOW Magazine, Canada's largest alternative newsweekly. He was also a founding editor of writers' e-zine *IN* (*I*nkwell *N*ewswatch) and serves on the board of the Freelance Writers Organization-International (FWO, the fourth largest writers' database in the world, *IN*'s parent company) and still does intermittent freelance gigs. He is currently drummer for a handful of Toronto bands of various ilk. He also loves the NBA, R&B, TV, GQ, U of I, RFK, MLK, NYC, THC, SCT, Muhammad Ali, John Lennon and God.

Made in United States
North Haven, CT
26 June 2024

54086055R10135